S.O.E

Special Operations Executive

Best Beloved

A Necessary Woman

S.O.E.
Special Operations Executive

by

Deborah Clair

Best Beloved

by

Deborah Clair

A Necessary Woman

by

Deborah Clair and Philippa Urquhart

methuen & co

S.*O.E.* – *Special Operations Executive* and *Best Beloved*
First published in paperback in Great Britain by Methuen & Co. 2022

A Necessary Woman
First published in this collection in Great Britain by Methuen & Co. 2022

1

Methuen & Co
Orchard House
Railway Street
Slingsby, York, YO62 4AN

Methuen & Co. Limited Reg. No. 5278590

www.methuen.co.uk

A CIP catalogue record for this title is available from the British Library

ISBN: 978-0-413-77864-2

Typeset in Great Britain by SX Composing DTP, Rayleigh, Essex
Printed and bound in Great Britain by CPI Group (UK) Ltd, Croydon, CR0 4YY

Contents

S.O.E.
Special Operations Executive

S.O.E.
Special Operations Executive

by

Deborah Clair

To Vera and to Noor and all those who didn't come through.
And to my H.Q.: Daniel, Niamh and Esme

S.O.E.

Special Operations Executive

Characters

Vera Atkins (1908–2000)	Intelligence Officer for the Special Operations Executive, Baker Street, London
Noor Inayat Khan (Nora Baker) (1914–44)	Special Operations Executive Wireless Operator for the CINEMA Circuit, Paris
Hans Josef Kieffer (1900–47)	Head of the German Secret Police, *Der Sicherheitsdienst*, Avenue Foch, Paris

Cast

Vera Atkins	Deborah Clair
Noor/Nora	Natasha Jayahendry
Hans Josef Kieffer	Tim Marriott

Creative Team

Director	Dominique Gerrard
Designer	Dee Harvey
Lighting Designer	Cat Alchin
Stage Manager	Suzan O'Sullivan
Aftershow presentations	Professor Juliette Pattinson & Dr Kate Vigurs
Producers	Deborah Clair and Nicholas Collett

A note about staging

The train carriage (p. 28) can be depicted by arranging the two chairs to face each other. The sliding door is mimed.

The bench (p. 46) can be formed by pushing the two chairs together.

Bibliography

Sarah Helm, *A Life in Secrets – The story of Vera Atkins and the Lost Agents of SOE* (London 2006)

Shrabani Basu, *Spy Princess – The Life of Noor Inayat Khan* (Gloucestershire 2008)

Juliette Pattinson, *Secret War – A Pictorial Record of the Special Operations Executive* (London 2001)

Kate Vigurs, *Mission France – The True History of the Women of SOE* (London 2021)

Special thanks to Fabrice Boedt and Alexiane Boedt for their kind help with my French and German translations.

Scene One

[*Blackout*

[*Sound of an old-fashioned projector wheel can be heard*]

Vera Atkins, *now nearly eighty years of age, is being interviewed for the Imperial War Museum Archive. She sits in a chair – lit from the front so she appears in silhouette – smoking a cigarette.*

Vera I think we assessed the chances of coming through at no more than fifty per cent. I think . . . some thirty per cent were in fact arrested and went through the camps . . . And probably we lost about ten per cent, fifteen per cent maybe. I went out to War Crimes in er . . . January '46 in order to trace what had happened to people who one didn't know . . . whose fate one didn't know or . . . the details of what happened to them, what *had* happened to them.

[*A memory of* **Kieffer**, *the Head of the German Secret Police, at his interrogation appears over* **Vera***'s left shoulder.* **Kieffer** *is in civilian clothes*]

Lights up on **Kieffer**

Kieffer [*leaning forwards conspiratorially*] I'll tell you a secret. [**Vera** *leans in cautiously*] There is nothing I like more than to hear English spoken . . . with a proper English accent.

Vera [*trying to ignore this voice from the past*] Accompany the agents out to the field, see them off, see them into their planes. Do a final security check on them to see that they didn't go off with English money in their pockets or whatever. You'd check and the realisation that they were going out on a very dangerous mission and that this was quite possibly the last glimpse they had of the lovely countryside through which you were travelling with them.

Kieffer And you remained quite safely at your end.

Vera [*responds to* **Kieffer***'s voice*] Safe as bombs would let you be.

Kieffer Although . . . the *burden* of responsibility was on the person . . . who was seeing them off . . . no?

[*Lights fade on* **Vera** *and* **Kieffer**

[*Projection of a placard: a bare upstairs room near S.O.E. H.Q., Baker Street, June 1943*]

[*Projection of a placard appears:* **Vera**]

Enter **Vera**

[*Lights up on* **Vera**, *an Englishwoman in her late thirties – dressed in a simple Forties style jacket and skirt – who is both friendly and formal*]

Enter **Noor**

[*Lights up on* **Noor**, *a young Indian woman in her late twenties – dressed in a simple Forties style blouse and skirt – who appears a little nervous*]

Vera Ah, Noor! Noor Inayat Khan . . .

Noor Miss Atkins.

[*Lights up on a bare stage and two door frames upstage with a silk screen hung between them, a blackboard on a stand, three wooden crates, two rickety chairs and a small table*]

Vera You remember me?

Noor Of course.

Vera Good. I wondered if you would.

Noor I do.

Vera You see, I understand that you have rather a lot to remember at the moment.

Noor I couldn't forget you, Miss Atkins.

Vera Indeed. Well, I'll take that as a compliment . . . if rather a back-handed one.

Noor It's just . . .

Vera . . . Yes?

Noor I'm going by the name of Nora Baker these days. Beaulieu's suggestion.

Vera Yes, of course. Well, you'll have many names . . .

Noor Yes, Miss Atkins and I'll remember them all.

Vera [*their eyes meet, suddenly serious*] And so will I.

[*Pause*]

Vera [*smiling*] Come with me. [**Vera** *moves upstage.* **Noor** *follows*] How was Bristol?

Noor I think it went well, Miss Atkins.

Vera So I gather. Book research. Was a good cover.

Noor [*proudly*] Collecting impressions of air raids from children . . . for the BBC. I even visited a school.

Vera And I detect, something you'd be more than happy doing . . . in reality.

Noor [*nodding, shyly*] You've guessed.

Vera Well, Major Buckmaster thought that all worked a treat. And – if anyone checked – not entirely without foundation. I understand you were a writer of children's stories in France?

Noor Oh . . . er . . . just beginning really . . .

Vera Nonsense! The Major says you were a published author, on the wireless and everything in Paris. Mentions it every time your name comes up.

[*Pause as* **Noor** *struggles to form a swift answer*]

Noor That is true, but it is something I have . . . locked away. Another life, another . . . realm.

Vera Realm? [*Pause*] Indeed it is. Quite so. [*Grabs a handful of papers from the desk and quickly changes the subject*] Well, I must say, the Bristol report seems excellent in many aspects. [*Reviewing the report*] Setting up of live letterboxes . . . both locations . . . very suitable: MET. Dead letterboxes . . . both locations very suitable: MET. Recruitment of contacts . . . candidates well-chosen and reliable: MET. Selection of suitable secure premises for wireless transmission: MET. SOE Officer's remarks are: 'Agent has worked very hard and I consider this quite a good scheme . . .' Hmmm. [*Frowning*] Rather a – measured – overall assessment after all that praise.

Noor [*sighing*] But . . .

Vera But what?

Noor I'm sorry. Please continue, Miss Atkins.

Vera [*resumes reading report*] Oh, I see. [*Reading further*] Yes. Yes. Well, I must say I hardly consider this insurmountable.

Noor [*forgetting herself*] It was terrible! I was petrified!

Vera I'd be concerned if you weren't . . .

Noor Even though it wasn't real!

Vera And that was its purpose . . . a practice interrogation . . .

Noor And when I did speak, I made stupid mistakes. Gave too much away.

Vera Nora, mistakes are training so as not to make them in the field.

Noor I'm too emotional! [*Gesturing to the report*] I know that's what it says . . .

Vera That too . . . not entirely bad.

Noor Because of my father, you know?

Vera Yes. I do. But Sufism is something I can claim to know very little about.

Noor He was man of great wisd . . .

Vera [*curtly*] And that does not concern me here, neither should it you. Understood?

Noor Yes, Miss Atkins.

Vera Now, I have been asked by Major Buckmaster to show you this. [*Takes a handwritten letter from her breast pocket.* **Noor** *eyes it suspiciously*] It's a letter written from two women, fellow students of yours at Chorleywood. Read it now please.

[**Noor** *takes the letter, her hands shaking*]

Vera Take your time.

Noor [*reading. After a few moments she looks up at* **Vera**] I do not agree with what this letter says. [**Noor** *hands the letter back to* **Vera**]

Vera Go on.

Noor [*visibly hurt by the letter's contents*] These women have made judgements about my character, my . . . suitability as an agent . . . without truly knowing me or my capabilities. What they cannot know is my resolve to be like the King of Benares as he looked upon the broken body of the tortoise in the courtyard of his palace . . .

Vera From your book?

Noor Yes, Miss Atkins.

Vera Do you know why you're here?

Noor [*sighing*] I have felt desperate all the way on the train. I am convinced that I am about to be turned out.

Vera And why would you think you're about to be . . . RD'd?

Noor Because of what happened in Bristol; the police interrogation. Now this letter.

Vera Treat the interrogation like any other exercise. Review, revise, repeat or reject.

Noor You're not turning me out?

Vera You're way beyond that, Noor. [*Pause*] Paris have sent an SOS. We need you to be one of a handful of wireless operators we still have left in the city. You'd be joining CINEMA, a sub-circuit of PROSPER. You're here because you're a French native with outstanding wireless skills and *we* are the ones who are desperate. We're desperate for you, Noor. So much so that we can't even send you back to Thame to complete your training.

Noor It doesn't matter . . . I don't mind . . . I'm ready.

Vera Yes, we think so too. [*To* **Noor**'*s surprise* **Vera** *suddenly tears the letter in half and burns it in an ashtray*] Now, no more distractions. Major Buckmaster has asked me to prepare you for the field while we wait for a full moon. [**Noor** *looks at* **Vera**] It has to be that way. Can't send you in daylight and the pilot has to be able to see where to land. But first we must deal with any loose ends here.

Noor Loose ends?

Vera Your ties, your family . . .

Noor I see.

Vera Of course, we have already been doing this for months. Remind me, what have you told them?

Noor That I'm going away to do an important job. They don't know I'm returning to France. I think my mother was reassured by my uniform when I last went home.

Vera Uniform?

Noor She noticed the khaki for the FANYs and that the WAAF blue was gone. My mother believes I am likely to come to less harm if I am in the nursing core.

Vera I see. Well, we have to do what we have to do to disguise our intentions. Can you live with that lie?

Noor I have not lied. I have just let my mother see what she wishes to see.

Vera It is very important to you . . . telling the truth?

Noor It is.

Vera I do wonder how that will work with being an SOE agent?

Noor I think I have found a way to make it work.

Vera I'm glad to hear it. Just keep your wits about you. Even though you lived in Paris for most of your life, the city is not what it was, even two years ago.

Noor I can assure you a long shadow was already cast over my country in June '40 when I fled with my family, Miss Atkins.

Vera Well we'll go through my list later. It's compiled from the most up-to-date information we have coming out of the capital and the provinces. Some things may seem rather trivial, such as – I don't know – remembering not to order a café au lait.

Noor Why's that?

Vera There's no such thing. No longer sufficient supplies of milk . . . or sugar for that matter.

Noor I see.

Vera Do you drink? [**Noor** *shakes her head*] All right, well even if you order for someone else the Germans have banned the sale of alcohol on Sundays. Place an order on the wrong day and it could be your last. Do you smoke?

Noor A little.

Vera You'll have to ask a male contact to buy your cigarettes.

Noor You're joking!

Vera I wish I was. Honestly, I wouldn't last five minutes! Joking aside though, this all may seem very trivial, but a tiny slip-up could cost your life and the lives of your fellow agents. If you're not a hundred per cent certain in a situation, err on the side of caution.

Noor Yes, Miss Atkins.

Vera Now . . . your Will.

Noor All in order, Miss Atkins.

Vera Salary payments?

Noor To my Lloyds account, please. I believe you already have the details.

Vera Indeed I do.

Noor You have ensured my mother will have access to my money? And in the event of . . . if I do not return?

Vera I have. She will, of course. Paperwork's all filled out.

Noor Will you write . . .?

Vera I will do whatever you wish.

Noor . . . to my mother?

Vera It's our duty, our honour, to assist you . . .

Noor I would appreciate that.

Vera . . . minimise the suffering of your loved ones . . .

Noor Thank you.

Vera . . . while you are in the field.

[*Silence as the women pause to contemplate what* **Noor** *is about to do*]

Vera [*suddenly*] I think you should write a few lines now. [**Vera** *pulls a desk drawer open and takes out paper and a pen and slams them in front of* **Noor**]

Noor [*picking up the pen*] Now?

Vera No time like the present. A few lines now. To your mother.

[**Vera** *moves away from the desk.* **Noor** *thinks for a moment, but is struggling*]

Noor [*distressed*] I . . . don't know what to say . . .! What should I write? What does one say?!

Vera [*stepping in*] It's all right. All right. You wouldn't be the first to struggle with this . . .

Noor I *could* say: 'I'm thinking of you as I write these lines in the face of what I'm about to do . . .'

Vera Hmm. Rather portentous. Would joining the nursing core carry such a threat of danger?

Noor No, of course not and my return to nursing is what we must make sure she continues to believe. I never imagined writing to my mother would be this difficult. What on earth can I write?

Vera Platitudes. It won't matter. Keep it light. Keep it factual . . . What's the weather like? Tell her you're keeping busy. [**Noor** *begins to write, while* **Vera** *watches over her shoulder*] These words will be from you, written in your own hand. She'll treasure them forever.

[**Noor** *finishes the letter and signs her name at the bottom*]

Noor There. [**Noor** *hands the letter to* **Vera** *who seals it in an envelope and tucks it away*]

Vera This needn't be your last and only. Post is delivered by Lysander. We have a man on the ground in Paris.

Noor I see.

Vera Now, something more practical. Your cover story. Tell me who you are?

Noor My name is Jeanne-Marie Renier.

Vera Right. [*Points to herself*] Not Miss Atkins. I'm Gestapo. [*With a new hardness*] Where are you from?

Noor I was born in Blois.

Vera Funny accent. Let's see your papers. [**Noor** *hands* **Vera** *her fake identity card*] This is a new card. Where did you say you were from?

Noor I have recently arrived from Bordeaux. I got a new identity card there when I was looking for work in '43.

Vera Why were you in Bordeaux?

Noor My job?

Vera Which is?

Noor I'm a children's nurse.

[**Vera** *holds the ID card up to* **Noor***'s face so she can scrutinize both*]

Vera Why are you in Paris?

Noor Again, my job. I am looking for work.

Vera All right piss off, I'm bored now. Unless you fancy a . . .?

Noor [*quickly*] No, thank you.

Vera [*handing the ID card back to* **Noor**] Of course, we should have really done that in French. *Dois-je vous tester sur votre français? J'espère que non!*

Noor *Pas du tout! Je préfère parler en anglais tant que je le peux encore. Ça va me manquer.*

Vera Very well. [**Vera** *holds a small suitcase aloft*] This your wireless set?

Noor It is.

Vera I must say they've done well with the weight of that. You're only a slip of a thing after all. Mark II is it?

Noor Yes. I'm very grateful for the modification.

Vera This won't go with you; it'll be dropped a few days later. Pistol in here too?

Noor All I need.

[**Noor** *reaches to take the case before* **Vera** *thinks to open it*]

Vera Well that'll need to come out to take on the plane and remember that gets buried.

Noor As soon as I land.

Vera You'll only need it if . . .

Noor Gestapo have organised a welcome party.

Vera Exactly. Leo Marks has given you your codes? Know all your checks?

Noor True checks, bluff checks.

Vera I'll be watching the boards all the time for 'NURSE.'

Noor Or 'MADELEINE.'

Vera Well, we have a few more things to go through before Major Buckmaster will be down to wish you luck and no doubt hand you your gold compact.

Noor Gold compact?

Vera Chaps gets cufflinks, ladies get compacts. Something to remind you of us . . . and home.

Noor I see.

Vera Sort of the best and the worst part all rolled into one.

Noor It will be good to see Major Buckmaster again.

Vera [*composing herself*] Now for the part I don't like very much at all. [*She takes a matchbox out of her pocket and holds it aloft. She speaks in a matter-of-fact way rather like a doctor prescribing medication*] One matchbox, four compartments, four pills. [*Opening the matchbox she shows* **Noor** *the first compartment*] This one I like. Slip this is an SS Officer's tea . . . he'll be out like a light for six hours.

Noor Very good.

Vera Thought you'd like that. [*Pointing to the second compartment*] This one, the second, is for *you* – Benzedrine to keep you awake. Maybe you're on the run and dog-tired but need to stay alert. [*Pointing to the third compartment*] This, number three, will give you a dicky tummy.

Noor The point would be . . .?

Vera Faking an illness might just get you out of tight spot. One never knows.

Noor Yes.

Vera The fourth is your 'L' pill. Cyanide. You see it has a rubber coating? No point in swallowing, it has to be bitten. I hope you never have need of it, but if the net closes in and you don't fancy interrogation and torture . . .

Noor A way out . . . if I'm . . . frightened.

Vera [*closing the matchbox and passing it to* **Noor** *then suddenly covering* **Noor***'s hand with hers*] Noor, do whatever you can. Outclass, outwit, outrun them, kick, bite, scream, kill. 'L' is the last option.

Noor [*nodding*] Yes, Miss Atkins.

Vera Vera.

Noor Vera.

[*Pause*]

Vera [*business-like again*] Let's have a look at your clothes [**Vera** *gestures for* **Noor** *to turn around*] Are these your own?

Noor The skirt is from Margaret Street, the blouse is my own.

Vera The blouse has the collar set in the French style. Buttons – work very well. The skirt is a good copy. We'll stitch in a French label. Anything in your pockets? Any English money? [**Vera** *moves closer to check* **Noor**'*s pockets*]

Noor No pockets! [*Catching sight of* **Vera**'*s brooch*] Such a pretty brooch. Is it a lapwing?

Vera It is. [**Vera** *unpins the brooch*] And now it's yours [*She pins the brooch onto* **Noor**'*s blouse, then stops and frowns*] Strange. [**Vera** *steps back slowly and looks directly at* **Noor** *who now has a mystical air*]

Noor You know.

Vera [*unsure of herself for the first time*] Do I?

Noor Yes. [*Pause*] Tell me, when did you realise?

Vera Oh, only just now.

Noor I could have sworn you knew earlier.

Vera When I pinned on that brooch. The lapwing.

Noor I suppose it doesn't matter much.

Vera I've been . . . searching for you.

Noor And you've been doing very well; you've almost found me.

Vera You were captured . . .

Noor Yes.

Vera By the *Sicherheitsdienst* . . . the secret police.

Noor Yes.

Vera And tortured . . .

Noor Yes.

Vera . . . and . . .

Noor That shouldn't stop us . . .

Vera No?

Noor . . . finding the truth.

[*Sound of morse code crackles through the air*]

[*Lights fade to black*

Scene Two

[*Darkness*]

[*Sound of an old-fashioned projector wheel can be heard*]

[**Vera Atkins**, *now nearly eighty years of age, is being interviewed for the Imperial War Museum Archive. She sits in a chair – lit from the front so she appears in silhouette – smoking a cigarette*]

[*Sound of* **Vera Atkins** *' Imperial War Museum 1987 archive recording*]

Vera Well, one of the nicest things was always to see returning agents and . . . and this was extremely agreeable because . . . seeing them off was always as a strain, a considerable strain and some three hours later you'd be on the tarmac welcoming back people who had returned so you turned yourself inside out. And then you'd get their stories and it was from them that one heard what had happened to those who had *not* returned, gave you a lead to what had happened. When a person was arrested, you did *not* know what had happened to them subsequently, you were not in touch with them any longer, you did not know where they were sent or what had happened, whether they were alive or whether they were dead and, er, therefore the returning agents with the information which they brought was more than interesting and more than harrowing. It's very difficult to explain these things to people who are *not* connected and it's very difficult to recreate the atmosphere of these days . . .

[*Projection of a placard: January 1947, Allied Occupied Germany*]

[*Projection of a placard:* **Noor**]

[*Sound of a train pulling out of a station and a German guard announcing the station stops*]

[*Lights up on a train carriage*]

Enter **Vera**

[**Vera**, *holding a suitcase and with a package under her arm, is now dressed as a Squadron Officer, in her WAAF uniform.* **Vera** *stows her case, sets the package next to her and sits down. She takes out her case notes and starts to read*]

[*Train carriage door slides back*]

Enter **Noor**

[**Noor** *is wearing the same clothes as in Scene One and carrying the suitcase concealing her wireless transmitter. She sits down*]

Vera [*looking up from her notes*] You're back, I see.

Noor Chance to interrogate Kieffer. Honestly, I wouldn't miss this for the world. Tell me, where did you find him?

Vera He was hiding in plain sight.

Noor Oh yes?

Vera Working as a cleaner in a hotel in Garmisch Partenkirchen.

Noor [*laughing*] I say, bit of a fall from grace from being Head of the Secret Police at Avenue Foch!

Vera Indeed it is. [*Pause*] I suppose that's my specialism now.

Noor Investigations?

Vera Falls from grace and . . . seeing matters through to their necessary conclusion.

Noor What you're doing – the interviews, the interrogations of the main culprits – you're doing it for all of us, aren't you, Vera? All of your girls?

Vera I am. [*She buries her head back into her notes*] And it's the least I can do for you.

[*Pause*]

Noor You can ask me . . . if you want to.

Vera Ha! Somehow . . . it's worse.

Noor Oh?

Vera To ask you directly.

Noor I am sure you've imagined what happened.

Vera I have . . .

Noor So this is your chance to confirm your suspicions.

Vera I suppose so, but . . .

Noor Are you worried the truth might be too . . . unpalatable?

Vera No.

Noor Then what?

Vera That hearing the truth . . . from your lips . . . would be . . .

Noor Harrowing?

Vera Harrowing . . . and . . . an admission of failure, of *my* failure . . .

Noor [*suddenly*] Oh, don't worry about that Vera!

Vera To uncover it myself . . . but I *do* worry . . .

Noor The Gestapo took care of all of that. [*Pause*] You're off to interrogate Kieffer aren't you? Ask him about the *Nacht und Nebel Aktion.*

Vera [*translating*] Night and fog.

Noor It's where they *disappear* you. Of course, Kieffer will deny its existence. I'm actually rather amazed you have discovered this much; it's impressive.

Vera [*Pause*] I imagine it's the things you've seen, what you went through. You're not . . . as I remember you, Noor.

Noor I'm not.

[*Silence*]

Vera [*gesturing to the suitcase*] Got your Mark II still?

Noor It's as if it's glued to me.

Vera [*smiling*] The night you left you didn't seem frightened . . . you were . . . serene.

Noor I was. *It* was . . . the whole picture. When we said goodbye on the airfield and I walked towards the Lizzie, didn't feel like a mission, but the beginning of a new chapter. A chance to make my own unique contribution: Fighting for Britain to free France. [**Noor** *starts to move forward, away from* Vera *into an area of moonlight USC*] Rather like a play – we all had our parts – myself, the pilot, other agents, even you, Vera and Major Buckmaster back in England.

Vera This is the writer talking now, not the SOE agent.

Noor Perhaps. [*Pause*] Of course, there was fear. There were four of us . . . two in each plane. We were all frightened, but we masked it. Fear was the enemy and it wasn't going to help us. [*She begins to speak as she if she is in the moment*] I've met the pilot before, a tall chap with fair hair. He's handsome. [*She climbs onto a rostra, DSR*] Our eyes meet as I climb aboard – a connection we can't acknowledge. A noisy, rattling take-off and then before long we are over the Channel. Small planes . . . fly slowly and we're not allowed to communicate with each other. That's a long time to be with your own thoughts. The pilot knows I'm nervous so he suddenly does something remarkable. He is extremely kind: he talks to me, even though this is against protocol. We're waiting in the wings for the curtain to go up. Then suddenly the clouds part and there's France below. The pilot says: 'Now Madame, we are approaching your beautiful country. Isn't it lovely in the moonlight?'

Vera Black mark for that pilot, Germans might be listening . . .

Noor He's reaching out from the darkness, a bright beacon in a sea of loneliness. One human to another. I will not turn away or ignore this kindness. 'I think it is heavenly,' I reply. We steal past the occupied towns and cities that the pilot is careful to never fly directly over. Instead, he reads a precision pathway that follows the shine of rivers, steeples, roads and railway lines, while the world sleeps beneath. We are sandmen. 'Second to the right, and straight on till morning.' That, Peter told Wendy, was the way to Neverland . . .

Vera A fairy tale?

Noor Why not? This story has all the hallmarks of one . . . heroes, villains . . . [*Pause*] We creep past the city of Caen on our left, Alençon the same. Le Mans and Tours I know will be to the right, but they are too far off to make out. Soon we will be approaching our destination: a field north-east of Angers, five and a quarter kilometres south of Tierce, three and a half kilometres west-north-west of the little village of Villevêcque. We see the three lights ahead, an inverted L shape, our people on the ground below. And then the instruction from the cockpit: 'Prepare to land' and my heart, which was at times in my mouth, now skips a beat. We have practised the landing many times, but now I am dizzy with the reality that the moment has come. We hit the ground and fumble with our straps. The female agent in front of me . . .

Vera Cicely Lefort . . . died at Ravensbrück.

Noor I must pass down her case and then stow the luggage of those who were returning.

Vera [*reading from her notes*] Five came back on the return. Three political figures, two agents: Jack and Francine Agazarian.

Noor Finally, it's me. I descend the ladder and I'm met by GILBERT, head of the team on the ground.

Vera Alias Henri Dericourt. *L'homme qui fait le pick-up.* We'll come back to him.

Noor GILBERT'S assistant has bicycles for us . . . I must cycle to Angers train station to get to Paris. [**Noor** *is about to climb on her bicycle, when* **Vera** *moves forward, out of the train carriage, into* **Noor***'s reality*]

Vera Noor! Wait! Your pistol! [*She rushes over to* **Noor**, *facing her*] Bury . . . your . . . pistol!

Noor Didn't bring it.

Vera You . . .

Noor I am a pacifist!

Vera Noor!

Noor Sorry, I have to go and meet my contact in Paris. [*Repeating her instructions to herself*] Find CINEMA to assist PROSPER. [*Making to leave*] I'll send a message to H.Q. as soon as I can.

Vera Noor, what happened when you got to Paris?

Noor [*taking a moment to come back to the present*] There were only a few days.

Vera What do you mean?

Noor I made it to the address I was given in my instructions.

Vera Report to: Head of CINEMA Circuit.

Noor 40 rue Erlanger, Paris.

Vera Seize E Arrondissement.

Noor Eighth Floor.

Vera Opposite the lift door.

Noor [*repeating*] Opposite the lift door.

Vera Noor, remember the importance of retaining the little details.

Noor Yes.

Vera Better to look sure of yourself. That you've been here before, rather than a stranger arriving for the first time.

Noor Yes . . . I knock on the door.

Vera Who answered? Was he there?

Noor She.

Vera She?

Noor I don't know why, but I was expecting a woman –

Vera You thought CINEMA was a woman?

Noor Yes, an old one. I'd brought flowers.

Vera Why would you think that?

Noor I don't know. Just what I imagined.

Vera Who answered the door?

Noor . . . Gary Cooper.

Vera *Gary Cooper?* The . . . *the film actor?*

Noor His double . . . [*In the moment again*] He's . . . very handsome. [*She blushes*]

Vera Keep your focus.

Noor [*not listening*] I manage to stammer: 'I think I am expected.' He invites me inside. It a small apartment, sparse, quite pokey. We stand there a moment not knowing what to say . . .

Vera Well . . . you know what to say . . . give him the password!

Noor It's all rather awkward. He invites me to sit down. [**Noor** *sits*]

Vera All right. Now for the password. You come to ask about the building society for your friend Antoine.

Noor I sit with the flowers on my lap. We wait. I can sense another person in the kitchen at the back. Perhaps this is the old woman?

Vera [*sighing*] Entirely your own invention.

Noor A woman appears from the kitchen, but she's young . . . his girlfriend, wife? She offers to make us coffee.

Vera At which point you abandoned the notion of the old woman. Give him the password!

Noor He asks if I am his contact from London.

Vera Good. He really shouldn't have had to.

Noor Then I give the password . . .

Vera *Yes?*

Noor *Je viens de la part de votre ami Antoine pour des nouvelles au sujet de la société en Bâtiment.*

Vera [*sighs*] Thank God.

Noor He replies: *L'affaire est en cours.* [*Pause*] So . . . *this* is CINEMA!

Vera Émile Henri Garry. Head of CINEMA, a sub-circuit of PROSPER.

Noor Not an old lady.

Vera *Not* an old lady . . . but yes, more than a passing resemblance to Gary Cooper. You'd better give him your carnations.

[*The two women laugh to dispel the tension*]

Noor That was the beginning. First days were a bit of a whirl. I was introduced to key members of PROSPER . . . the Paris Circuit. I'm not Noor or even Nora now, but Jeanne-Marie or MADELEINE. Over the next days I meet RENAUD . . .

Vera France Antelme. Code name: RENAUD. Cover name: Antoine Ratier. Head of BRICKLAYER Circuit. Killed at Gross-Rosen, September 1944.

Noor He's a tall Mauritian in his forties. RENAUD takes me under his wing. Shows me the new Paris of check points, German soldiers and Nazi flags. They've even renamed the streets, the cafés. My city is ailing. It has a cancer now that somehow we *must* cure. [*Pause*] I meet ARCHAMBAUD. The strangest thing. We went to the same school in Paris! I don't remember him.

Vera Gilbert Norman, PROSPER's wireless operator. Code name: ARCHAMBAUD. Killed at Mauthausen, September 1944.

Noor ARCHAMBAUD takes me to the National College of Agriculture at Grignon. As yet I have no wireless transceiver of my own, we head for the greenhouse in the college grounds. We enter – the smell of summer vegetation hits me. ARCHAMBAUD uncovers the wireless from its hiding place, in a basket covered in garden tools. I watch as he suddenly shins up a wooden ladder, positioned between the plants, to hook the sixty-foot long aerial into the rafters. [**Noor**'*s eyes follow upwards as she watches* ARCHAMBAUD *climb*] As I blink toward the sky, he is a god and . . . I have a sense that . . . anything is possible, that we will succeed. We can triumph. I feel . . . elated. [*Pause*] It's obvious why this is an excellent place to transmit. No time to waste. I hastily tap out a short message to H.Q.

[*Sound of morse code rattles through the air*]

Vera Buck and I were both watching the boards that day, but we weren't expecting you to start making your scheds so soon. [*Proudly*] The fastest response from any agent in the field post landing. The call-sign BUTCHER suddenly appears. And our minds leap to connect: BUTCHER – ARCHAMBAUD – Gilbert Norman, PROSPER'S wireless operator. Read your message word by word, as it was decoded.

Noor [*tapping out morse code*] NURSE . . . ARRIVED . . . HAPPY . . . AND . . . ALL RIGHT.

Vera [*reading first part of the message at the same time*] NURSE . . . ARRIVED . . . HAPPY . . . AND . . . ALL RIGHT. DAMAGED WT SET ON LANDING. SEND REPLACEMENT SOONEST. And then your hallmark sign-off: TALLY HO! Relief all round. I swear Buck and I almost kissed.

Noor You did?

Vera 'course not. [*Pause*] We were worried about you . . . and then we were happy.

Noor I worked at Grignon until my wireless arrived. [*With effort*] You may as well know. I made two mistakes.

Vera With transmissions?

Noor With my . . . tea-making.

Vera Tea?

Noor I put the milk in first. Madame Balachowsky at the college said that was too English.

Vera She's right! Noor, it may seem trivial, but the tiniest of details . . .

Noor That was the first error.

Vera The second?

Noor Far more grave . . .

Vera Go on.

Noor My portfolio of security codes . . .

Vera What about it?

Noor I left it.

Vera Where?

Noor The entrance hall . . . of the Agricultural College.

Vera Noor!

Noor It was recovered.

Vera By whom?

Noor Professor Balachowsky. It was all right. He and his wife were part of everything. Sub-agents. And . . . I learned my lesson, a valuable one. The Professor told me that it's best to conduct myself as if everyone around me was a spy. The Gestapo are everywhere.

Vera He's right! Noor, you *know* this.

Noor It's very different when you're there . . . in the field! The loneliest of the loneliest of jobs. It meant something to have made connections, however brief . . . or tenuous. [*Pause*] That was day I met PROSPER.

Vera Francis Suttill, cover name: François Desprez, code name: PROSPER, Head of the Circuit.

Noor We all had Sunday lunch together.

Vera *Together?*

Noor Myself, the Balachowskys, ARCHAMBAUD, DENISE, PROSPER, the Vanderwyckts . . . and er . . . two others. [*Pause*] I didn't realise it at the time, but I think that day I was happy. Maybe it was the only day.

Vera Noor, you said earlier: There were only a few days?

Noor That's right. There were [*she counts in her head*] six.

Vera Six days until what?

Noor The fall . . . the fall of PROSPER.

[*Sudden burst of gunfire and shouting in the street outside.* **Noor** *and* **Vera** *immediately sink to the floor to take cover*]

Vera What is that?! What's . . .?

Noor It's just a raid. [*She peers out of the window*] You'll get used to them.

Vera What's happening?

Noor It's either Gestapo rounding up Jews or Gestapo rounding up resistance fighters.

Vera Where will they take them?

Noor Somewhere they won't come back from.

Vera None ever return?

Noor No. [*Pause*] The resistance might go to Avenue Foch first for . . . questioning. If that's deemed useful by the *Sicherheitsdienst.*

Vera Is that what happened with PROSPER?

Noor Was a chain of events. But I suppose the first sign was the parachute drop near Grignon. PROSPER had arranged it on the night of 21st June.

Vera I remember. That was the request for arms and your personal effects. Your Mark II as well.

Noor Well the arms and the Mark II were fine . . .

[*A suitcase suddenly drops from above and scatters clothing all over the ground,* **Vera** *and* **Noor** *scramble to retrieve the clothing*]

Noor It was no one's fault, just one of those things, but one of the 'shutes came down on a tree. My clothes were everywhere. PROSPER and the reception committee had to work all night to retrieve every item.

Vera Of course there could be no evidence.

Noor There was also an agent being dropped . . . JACQUOT?

Vera George Connerade. Code name JACQUOT.

Noor All that was found was his suitcase and a neatly folded parachute. I just got a sense from that evening. A sixth sense . . .

Vera Of what?

Noor Things . . . unravelling.

Vera From that point?

Noor You have to appreciate how sudden the next events are.

Vera Do you remember what happened next?

Noor One doesn't always hear, can't know everything.

Vera That's fine. You're not supposed to.

Noor Things get muddled.

Vera [*holding her hands up in a triangle shape*] The core of a circuit is three – Organiser, courier, wireless operator.

Noor Yes. [*In training mode again*] They should meet or be seen together . . . as little as possible.

Vera Indeed.

Noor They met.

Vera Who?

Noor All the time.

Vera Who? Noor – who?

Noor PROSPER, DENISE, ARCHAMBAUD . . .

Vera Where?

Noor Restaurants . . . the *same* café in Montmartre. I knew it wasn't right! RENAUD said they'd play poker and sometimes spoke in English.

Vera My God!

Noor PROSPER was brilliant! He was! So successful and he did so much for the cause. People were in awe.

Vera The chain of events?

Noor I can only give you my version.

Vera Yes.

Noor We were preparing for the Allied invasion. When I arrived, there was already a momentum. Felt it was coming. PROSPER was all over the place – meeting with sub-circuits, arranging arms drops. The trouble was, so were the Germans. New roadblocks were springing up everywhere and they had evidence. Resistance activity. They'd found exploded containers from drops. Must have intercepted some information because within twenty-four hours PROSPER, DENISE, ARCHAMBAUD – all three – were gone and the whole bloody thing was blown!

Vera How did you find out?

Noor [*she begins to retrace her steps*] First I knew was on the morning of the twenty-fourth. I had a meeting with ARCHAMBAUD. Planned to stay at the college a couple of days, send some transmissions from the greenhouse. I went to his friend's apartment where we usually met, but no one there. I went on to the college and waited. It's Friday afternoon. I'm feeling very anxious. I haven't eaten a thing all day. There's something not right, not right at all.

[**Noor** *paces the floor, looks about nervously*]

Vera What can you see?

Noor Nothing! No one's about. Much too quiet . . . wait, I can see . . . Professor Balachowsky. He's trying to look casual, but I can tell he's not calm. He's seen me and he's rushing towards me now across the courtyard. He pulls me into a side room. It's PROSPER he tells me, PROSPER, DENISE and fifteen others! He's speaking quietly, but very quickly. They've been arrested . . . they've been arrested he says and we must act . . . we must act immediately . . .

Vera What about ARCHAMBAUD?

Noor Escaped. He's . . . escaped! Got away! Yes? I hang on to this. ARCHAMBAUD . . . is my friend. We rush into the greenhouse and I seize the transmitter to find a new hiding place. Where? Where? Carry it in its suitcase into the vegetable garden. It's . . . heavy, the corners jabbing into my legs. We haven't brought a spade so now we're pulling . . . pulling at the earth . . . a lettuce bed . . . with our bare hands. Luckily, the summer soil is loose and powdery, but the hole must be big and the earth keeps sliding back in . . .

Vera Noor . . . is it done? Is it *done*?

Noor Yes . . . I'm on the train back to Paris [*Tries to slow her breathing*] Gestapo have boarded. I cover the dirt in my fingernails by making my hands into fists, in my lap.

Vera Sunday 25th June. London H.Q. receives a flash message out of the teleprinter in the Signals Room. I rush into the office from home. It comes from local F section recruits in Paris. PROSPER, ARCHAMBAUD, DENISE . . . DISAPPEARED BELIEVED . . . ARRESTED. [*To* **Noor**] You got back to Paris?

Noor [*nodding*] I contact Henri Garry, CINEMA. We go to RENAUD'S apartment to wait. We wait . . . all day. RENAUD returns around 10p.m. from Poitiers. We tell him PROSPER is blown. He tells Garry to lay low and finds a safe house for me.

Vera 1 Square Malberbe, Paris. Madame Aigrain. It's in RENAUD'S file.

Noor On Sunday I return to Grignon to find out how the news of the arrests, reached the Balachowskys. The Professor meets me at the door, barring any further entrance. A phone call to my wife, he says. *N'approchez pas!* He's speaking in a low voice again. Ignore us. For your own safety. *N'approchez pas!* Stay away . . . stay away!

Vera Where next? Back to the safe house?

Noor Yes. I hear that RENAUD has asked colleagues in the circuit to attend the apartments of DENISE and ARCHAMBAUD. She's not been seen since Wednesday. They check ARCHAMBAUD's place. He shares it with Nicholas Laurent and his wife.

Vera ARCHAMBAUD's bicycle was against the wall. His room was very tidy, Sheets folded, clothes in the wardrobe.

Noor The Laurents' room is another story. Drawers half open, clothes taken out in a hurry. Food on the stove.

Vera A raid?

Noor Perhaps. Or they left in a hurry.

Vera Is that when you knew . . . about ARCHAMBAUD?

Noor One never gives up hope.

Vera Nothing on the board from BUTCHER in days. Must be true.

Noor Time goes on though, hope wanes. [*Pause*] Garry and his fiancée get married. I attend. RENAUD stays away. The Garrys go back to Le Mans.

Vera What next?

Noor RENAUD's old flat. The concierge says that the Gestapo have been. Tall men. They bully her and describe RENAUD perfectly. Where is Ratier? Antoine Ratier?

Vera Becoming pretty anxious to get you both out. Buck's turning cartwheels.

Noor Meeting between myself, RENAUD and two local recruits – Gieules and Savy. RENAUD knows it's dangerous now to stay. Working to get him and Savy out; Savy's in danger too. The College at Grignon is now occupied, Prof Balachosky is gone. They're rounding up students to gather information. The Gestapo march them into the forest in groups of ten. Threaten them and fire shots in the air to spook the rest. RENAUD and I retreat to Robert Benoist's estate at Auffargis near Rambouillet. We burn papers and codes. Prepare RENAUD's evacuation by Lysander. GILBERT is organising the flight. RENAUD is keen that I should become GILBERT's wireless operator when he departs. GILBERT needs an operator and RENAUD thinks he'll, in turn, be a good guide for me.

Vera Not if I have anything to do with it.

Noor RENAUD, leaves me 30,000 francs to cover my costs and those of the circuit. We've been in hiding for two weeks, I will miss him when he leaves. He tells me his real name is France. He's divorced and has two young boys. We say we'll meet after the war, but we both know we won't. Just a feeling . . . I don't know.

Vera RENAUD, or France Antelme, arrives back for debriefing on 20th July. Antelme is proud and resilient, but this is not the man we sent to Paris a few months ago. He's shaken. He informs us of the current picture – following the fall of PROSPER – the scramble to close down letterboxes, abandon safe houses, destroy paperwork. The Gestapo have raided PROSPER's arms depots. Resistance members . . . many farmers . . . who have let drops happen on their land are being rounded-up. There's talk of a deal, a pact . . . if they co-operate, they'll be treated as soldiers not traitors for execution . . .

Noor [*sitting with her Mark II*] RENAUD is gone.

Vera [*in the signals room, waiting for news*] No communication from ACHAMBAUD for days. And then . . . 7th July, the code: butcher suddenly appears on the board. [*Sound of morse code*] He confirms PROSPER's capture, but he, ARCHAMBAUD, is free?

[*Lights slow fade over the next sequence of lines to leave* **Vera** *and* **Noor** *in two spotlights, SR and SL*]

Noor [*psyching herself up*] I am alone.

Vera Something odd though . . . with BUTCHER'S message . . .

Noor Down to me now.

Vera Analysts raising issues . . .

Noor Can I do it?

Vera *Fist* . . . out of character . . .

Noor Know all my scheds . . .

Vera Strange . . . unlike his other traffic . . .

Noor All my codes . . . all my checks . . .

Vera Bluff check present, true check missing

Noor The ending?

Vera A flustered man . . .

Noor The unknown?

Vera Doing his first transmission . . .

Noor MADELEINE . . .

Vera Under protest.

Noor Poste MADELEINE begins . . .

Vera [*desperately*] Noor, you must know, this wasn't expected of you. We wanted to get you back! Why wouldn't you let us bring you home?

Noor There was only *me* left. ARCHAMBAUD was gone! His wireless buried! How on earth was London going to know what was going on?

Vera The enormity of it . . . what you offered us. All the German listening apparatus would now be trained on you –

Noor *I* am the last link!

Vera What we didn't know is they knew about you already. They even had a name: MADELEINE.

Noor I'll remain . . . and I'll rebuild the circuit.

Vera We sign the message off with: 'MAY GOD KEEP YOU.'

[*Spotlights slow fade*]
[Je Sens en Moi *by Germaine Sablon is played*]
[*Interval*]

Scene Three

[*Darkness*]

[Je Sens en Moi *by Germaine Sablon resumes*]

[*Lights up on* **Noor** *waiting nervously on a park bench, looking back and forth*]

Noor A new chapter begins. I'm still wearing your brooch, Vera. But now I *become* the lapwing. The female lapwing builds her nests on the ground, just as the SOE agent builds their *Réseau*; the French word for network, literally a 'nest.' Myself and three French agents – Gieules, Arrighi and Vaudevire. We meet several times a week at a bench at Tuileries Gardens to rebuild our nest. Then there's Viennot, a local businessman, he's always helpful. He's part of the Resistance, but he's friendly with the Germans. Does what he can to get information from Avenue Foch, the headquarters of the German secret police. All arrested agents go to Avenue Foch, none are seen again. A group of Lapwings . . . is known as a deceit.

Vera We send Nicholas Bodington over to assess the damage to the PROSPER Circuit, Jack Agazarian returns as his wireless operator. Henri Déricourt – GILBERT – arranges the reception. We ask ARCHAMBAUD to arrange a safe rendez-vous . . . it will be a test.

Noor Bodington and Agazarian decide to draw lots for who goes to meet ARCHAMBAUD. Agazarian is arrested as soon as he knocks on the door. I now act as wireless operator for Boddington, I send his messages.

Vera Noor, please be careful! We've lost six wireless operators already to the Gestapo. The Gestapo have detection vans everywhere.

Noor Over August I am transmitting [*looks at* **Vera**] – cautiously – between 5.00pm and 5.30 p.m. I carry my wireless set around with me most of the time. It's heavy, but I am now used to its weight, I can make it seem as if the contents are lighter. I transmit everywhere. Arrighi or Vaudevire drive me out to the suburbs . . . Montrouge, Levallois, Noisy-le-Grand. I transmit about money and flights and arms. I transmit for everyone.

Vera Keep it short, never in the same place.

Noor I transmit quickly and never in the same place.

Vera No more than ten minutes . . . ten?

Noor I transmit for everyone and never in the same place. But, after a while I'm running out of locations. I have exhausted everything, asked everyone. I turn to old friends – my music teacher Henriette Rénie, the family doctor – Dr Jourdan and his wife. I transmit from the Jourdans' garden in their country house at Marly-le-Roi. Try and relax in the sunshine. Madame Jourdan is kind, but she says I look thinner, that I look tense.

Vera The Germans now had a description, knew what you looked like.

Noor I dye my hair red. I dye my hair blonde. Change the style, change my clothes. I have a flat in Boulevard Richard Wallace which is really a letterbox to pick up and send messages. I see Madame Jourdois, the concierge, she says I'm always, *always* in a rush. I pretend I'm a little dotty, bit forgetful. I think she knows, but she seems to think I'm a nice girl. It's evening now, but it's still light, I'm leaning out of the window of the flat. [*With effort*] Trying to hook the aerial of my wireless onto a tree in the street.

Vera [*watching* **Noor**] Noor is that wise?

Noor [*concentrating on the task*] No choice. This is urgent. I must contact London as soon as possible. Can't . . . quite . . . reach . . .

Vera Noor this is stupid! Whatever the message this is too much of a risk. You're risking your own life and the lives of your fellow agents!

Noor Ah, damn! [*Sound of the aerial clattering to the ground*]

Vera Go and get it!

Noor I rush down out of the flat, straight down the stairs. It's as if my legs won't move fast enough. Madame Jourdois is just coming out of her room – typical – we almost collide! '*Ahh Mademoiselle Renier! Toujours pressée . . . toujours pressée!*' '*Madame.*' I reply: '*Mon . . . mon chapeau vient de tomber par la fenêtre!*' Madame Jourdois raises her eyebrows, but this seems to satisfy her as to my haste. I rush out into the street . . .

Vera [*calling out of the flat window to* **Noor**] Noor . . . it's at the base of the lamppost, hurry!

Noor Got it! It actually might be easier from here.

Vera Noor! Oh Christ, he's seen you. [*Ducking her head back into the flat*]

Noor All of a sudden, I hear a voice with a distinct German accent behind me? '*Puis-je vous aider, mademoiselle?*' I spin around to see a young German officer. I try and give nothing away in my expression, but I know this is it. The end of the road. I hadn't imagined it would be like this. The officer gestures towards the aerial. There's no getting away from it. I hand it to him. My brain is reeling . . . everything's happening too fast. Can I say I have just found it on the ground? That'll only lead to more questions and now I realise this man – this German officer – lives in the same block of flats. He has seen me before. We have seen each other, quite often. And then, suddenly, a miracle. The young man smiles . . . a kind, broad, smile. He reminds me of the boys I went to college with. He starts to climb the tree, quickly, with the aerial tucked into his belt. He disappears amongst the branches and I think of ARCHAMBAUD climbing the ladder that day in the greenhouse at Grignon. It's only a few weeks, but it seems so long ago now. Then, the officer's back at my side on the ground, brushing the leaves off his uniform. '*Es ist jetzt hoch.*' He points upwards. '*Ich hoffe, das hilft Ihnen mit dem Signal? Um welche Funkstation handelt es sich?*' I have quite good German. He helps me further though. '*Für die Musik?*'

Vera He thinks you want to listen to music on the wireless. Go with it!

Noor '*Ahh . . . für den neuesten Tanz . . . den Jitter-Bug!*' [*She performs a few quick dance moves*] I thank him and wave coyly, stroll back inside.

Vera Bravo Noor! Utterly convincing! Hadn't realised . . . you're quite the actress!

[*Still dancing,* **Noor** *comes back into the apartment. She takes* **Vera***'s hands and they start dancing together.* **Noor** *leads. After a while they separate.* **Vera** *curtsies and* **Noor** *bows. They collapse onto their chairs laughing*]

Vera It must have been terrible, living on your nerves like that. Your letters home were always so cheerful. Never betrayed your true feelings. [**Vera** *opens and reads* **Noor***'s letter*]

Noor *Dear Miss Atkins (excuse pencil)*
Your bird has brought me luck. I remember you so often. You cheered me up so sweetly before I left. Lots of things have happened and I haven't been able to settle down properly. Still my contacts have started to be regular and I am awfully happy. I hope we shall soon be celebrating. In fact, I owe you a date.
Lots of love
Yours Nora.

Vera We were all so impressed at H.Q. You remained undetected for months. Flawless messages, every security check intact. You astonished all those who believed they knew you.

Noor Thank you. [*Pause*] I followed your advice, Vera. I was always on the move. Of course, good luck can't last forever, but it will soon be October and I'll be going back. [**Noor** *moves between four points on the stage with her suitcase, building sound of hundreds of morse code message flying through the air*]

Noor Garry's flat in Neuilly . . .

Vera Passwords . . .

Noor Boulevard Richard Wallace . . .

Vera Parachutes . . .

Noor Friend in Surenes . . .

Vera People . . .

Noor Madame Peineau in Bondy

Vera Planes . . .

Noor Neuilly . . .

Vera Passwords . . .

Noor Wallace . . .

Vera Parachutes . . .

Noor Surenes . . .

Vera People . . .

Noor Bondy . . .

Vera Planes.

Noor Neuilly

Vera Passwords . . .

Noor Wallace . . .

Vera Parachutes . . .

Noor Surenes . . .

Vera People . . .

Noor Please! The Gestapo are getting nearer every day. They tail me but I get away. They – Vaudevire and Arrighi – tell me I can't work, I can't *be* in Paris anymore. Vaudevire takes me to the station at St. Lazare and puts me on the train to Normandy: 'MADELEINE, I never want to see you again. Not in Paris. Don't come back here, please.'

Vera They're right. Come home Noor!

Noor I need a flight!

Vera Consider *that* done.

Noor Not until there's someone to fill my post here . . .

Vera Lay low until then . . .

Noor I can't . . .

Vera Consider *that* an order . . .

Noor How can I leave . . .

Vera How can you stay?

Noor I return to Paris. I meet Viennot who is always helpful. He buys me new clothes. I meet Vaudevire. He's shaking his head. 'I'm disappointed to see you back,' he says but tries to help arrange a passage to England, through a contact. Something's not right . . . feels like a trap. We avoid it . . . narrowly. I say goodbye to the Jourdans, Madame Peineau, Madame Aigrain and it's all fine, because I'm leaving, I'm leaving on 14th October. Yes. It's all arranged. *Au revoir, au revoir, merci, merci, merci mille fois!* I'm staying in a corner house on rue de la Faisanderie. It's a five minute walk from Avenue Foch. Some might say insultingly close. But in the eye of the storm, it's strangely calm. I was being tailed earlier by two Gestapo men. I eluded them. It's two hours later. I'm back at the flat, putting the key in the door. I enter.

Vera NOOR!!

Noor Someone – a man – grabs me from behind the door! He seizes my hands. I struggle. He's very strong.

Vera NOOR . . . WHAT CAN I DO!?

Noor He's close, so close I smell him. Smell the coffee and tobacco on his breath. I throw myself to the floor, he tumbles with me. A lamp crashes beside us.

Vera FIGHT NOOR, FIGHT!

Noor I can make noise, so much noise . . . someone will come running. I'll get away.

Vera Outclass . . . outwit . . . OUTRUN THEM!

Noor I BITE . . . I KICK . . . I SCREAM! I bite his wrists. There's blood. *His* blood. All over him, all over my pale blue dress. He's forced to release his grip.

Vera YES NOOR!

Noor I can't get away though I try. He pushes me onto the sofa. Puts his whole weight on top of me. Gets his gun out of his pocket, presses it to my cheek: 'I *will* shoot you,' he says. 'Keep still or I *will* shoot you.' He reaches for the telephone on the table next to the sofa. Makes a call, I presume to Kieffer. My assailant can barely speak he's so out of breath. I hear the German voice on the other end of the line . . . suddenly alive, animated, energised: '*Sie haben sie?* MADELEINE? *Ha! Bringe sie hierher, bringe sie hierher.*'

Vera They're taking you to Avenue Foch?

Noor Four more men arrive. One I later will come to know as Ernest Vogt, Kieffer's translator. They think I'm French and Kieffer doesn't speak it. They bundle me in a car and we go on the short drive to Avenue Foch. I can't believe it. I can't accept it. Kieffer greets me at the entrance. His excitement hasn't waned, only increased: 'MADELEINE?!' Then I translate in my head: 'I had to come and see for myself!' Although, his mood, his whole demeanour is obvious. That's it, he's won. I am the holy grail, the prize he's been searching for.

Vera What did you do then?

Noor It was getting to the point where what I could *do* now was extremely limited. What does one do, not do? How much does one comply, not comply? Speak . . . not speak? Kieffer asks them to take me up to the fifth floor and make me comfortable. We climb to the top, passing a guardroom, a storeroom, a bathroom. Then a flash in my mind.

Vera Yes?

Noor A bath.

Vera A *bath*?

Noor 'I'd like a bath . . . I want a bath . . . Look at me!' I say to the officers. 'I have blood in my hair, I'm tired. I want a bath.' An awkward pause, they don't know what to say. Then Vogt pipes up: 'OK, she's wants a bath. You heard. Let her have a bath!' They shuffle around to make this possible. I enter the bathroom, but the guards won't let me fully shut the door. I stage a temper tantrum: 'I want to undress and have a bath,' I scream. 'I WON'T TOLERATE YOU LOOKING AT ME!'

Vera Be careful, Noor . . .

Noor They let me close the bathroom door. I turn the taps on to run the bath, but I waste no time. Out the window onto the roof gutter that runs along the attic windows. Paris is far below and I'm up here with the birds. I am the Lapwing.

[**Noor** *and* **Vera** *standing on the edge together*]

Vera Noor, this is far too high . . .

Noor But still it would be . . .

Vera Too high to jump . . .

Noor A form of escape . . .

Vera [*firmly*] *No,* Noor.

Noor They took my pill away, Vera . . .

Vera Please . . .

Noor 'Madeleine . . . '

Vera Noor?

Noor 'Madeleine . . . ' It's Vogt. He's calling through the window. 'Madeleine, don't be silly. You will kill yourself. Think of you mother . . . dearest Amma! Give me your hand.' I'm in shock. Not because of the height or the danger or anything else. The adrenaline starts to seep from my body. How does he *know*? How does he *know* about my mother? How does he know my *name* for her? [*Turning to* **Vera**] Vera . . . ? [**Vera** *starts to move away from* **Noor** *and retreats slowly back to her seat in the railway carriage*] Vera . . . ? How does he know about my mother?

Vera *L'homme qui fait le pick-up.* The postman.

Noor GILBERT?

Vera Henri Déricourt [*Pause*] We suspect . . . we have suspected for some time now . . . that he was a double agent.

Noor *GILBERT* . . . But we trusted him, trusted him with everything . . .

Vera The drops, the flights, the receptions . . . the mail . . .

Noor [*pause, then with anger*] Was *anything* . . . *anything* real? [**Vera** *does not reply*] Is that why you're speaking to Kieffer?

Vera It's one of the questions we would like settled. There are others also . . . PROSPER, ARCHAMBAUD . . . *you.*

Noor [*pointing to the package* **Vera** *has next to her on the seat*] What's in the package?

Vera It's a uniform . . . always carry it with me . . . on such journeys.

Noor A uniform.

Vera Yes.

Noor And why would you need a uniform, Vera?

Vera It's the uniform . . . [*swallowing*] it's the uniform, I would have given you, had I found you . . . [*with effort*] . . . had I found you alive.

Noor You *have* found me . . . And you know the end. [*Pause*] Vera – for my part and for that of the other women . . . you can't help us . . . but they can't hurt us anymore. We're above it. We're beyond it. [*Pause*] You prepared me, Vera. Now all that remains is for me to prepare *you.* It won't be easy though. He's quite . . . tricky.

Vera Prepare me? Prepare me for what?

Noor Kieffer.

[*Blackout*

Scene Four (unabridged)

[*Darkness*]

[**Vera Atkins**, *now nearly eighty years of age, is being interviewed for the Imperial War Museum*

Archive. She sits in a chair – lit from the front so she appears in silhouette – smoking a cigarette]

[*Sound of* **Vera***'s voice from the Imperial War Museum sound archive recording (1987)*]

Vera Well, I was based with the legal section of War Crimes which was in Bad Oeynhausen, head of the British Army on the Rhine . . . and I worked from there. I was only interested in tracing . . . the people who had gone to concentration camps and who had not returned and to find out how and where they were killed and I assisted the prosecution in three war crimes trials.

[*Projection of a placard: January 1947, Allie Occupied Germany*]

[*Sound of the inside of a prison. Mens' voices, prison officers shouting orders, doors locking and unlocking*]

[*Projection of a placard:* **Kieffer**]

Enter **Vera**

[**Vera** *enters* **Kieffer***'s cell. She is holding a briefcase. She is still dressed as a Squadron Officer, in her WAAF uniform. The cell is empty. She wanders around the sparsely furnished room which contains a bed, a desk and a chair. On the desk is a German newspaper, a framed photograph of a smiling teenage girl and some paperwork.* **Vera** *checks her watch but there is still no sign of the occupant. She starts to rearrange the room for her interview, but there's only one chair at the desk. She starts to moves the chair to find the best position to hold the interview.*

[*Sound of footsteps along the corridor,* **Vera** *does not seem to hear however, focused on her task*]

Enter ***Kieffer***

[*A tall man appears framed in the doorway. He quickly steps inside and waits as the door is closed and locked behind him.* **Vera** *hears this and swivels around. She stands face to face with* **Kieffer**]

Kieffer *Kann ich Ihnen helfen?*

Vera [*clearly startled*] . . . Herr . . . Kieffer!

Kieffer *Jawohl?*

Vera *Mein Name ist* Squadron Officer Vera Atkins. I . . .

Kieffer I know who you are. Welcome to my humble abode. [*He smiles and gestures at the cell*] I'm sorry I was taking my exercise.

Vera *Ich bin im Auftrag des britischen* War Office *gekommen.*

Kieffer *Bitte.* [*Gesturing to the end of his bed, he sits in the chair by his desk*] *Nehmen Sie Platz.*

Vera *Vielen Dank. Möchten Sie lieber Englisch oder Deutsch sprechen?*

Kieffer *Beide* . . . both! [*Leaning forwards conspiratorially*] I'll tell you a secret. [**Vera** *leans in cautiously*] There is nothing I like more than to hear English spoken . . . with a proper English accent.

Vera Is that so?

Kieffer [*offers her a cigarette, lights his own*] Where do you hail from . . . Oxford . . . Cambridge?

Vera London.

Kieffer Ah.

Vera London and . . . Winchelsea from time to time.

Kieffer Winchelsea.

Vera Just along the coast . . . from Hastings.

Kieffer William der Eroberer.

Vera Yes, that's it.

Kieffer That was the French. [*He taps the desk*] Had you there.

Vera Quite so. [*Starting again*] I'm here from the War Office to ask you some questions. Colonel Buckmaster and I have . . .

Kieffer Buckmaster?

Vera Yes.

Kieffer A name I have heard many times. More revered than Churchill in my department.

Vera Will you help us?

Kieffer Madam, I have the upmost respect for the Colonel, for yourself and the people of your division. Berlin always attached extraordinary importance to the French Section, so much so that I was obliged to neglect the other resistance circuits. I will do anything I can to assist you in your investigations.

[**Vera** *is noticeably stunned by* **Kieffer***'s obvious sincerity*]

[*Pause*]

[*Recovering,* **Vera** *opens her briefcase, rummages through it for her notes and a pen.* **Kieffer** *watches her intently*]

Vera Well . . . I would like to begin with asking you about the capture of three of our agents starting from June '43. [*Still rummaging through her briefcase*]

Kieffer June '43.

Vera Yes.

Kieffer The agents?

Vera [*taking a file from her briefcase*] The first is *this* man. [*Opening the file and handing a photograph to* **Kieffer**, *she carefully stresses the military title as she continues*] *Major* Francis Suttill.

Kieffer [*looking at, but not touching, the photograph*] PROSPER.

Vera Yes, PROSPER, Head of the Circuit. I would like you to tell me what happened following his arrest.

Kieffer [*recalling*] PROSPER . . . was a real coup. I can't pretend to being anything else than absolutely over the moon when he was brought into Avenue Foch. You know there were three though . . . pillars of the circuit. DENISE the courier, ARCHAMBAUD the wireless . . . they were found together . . .

Vera *Together?*

Kieffer [*in a matter of fact way*] Yes. They were lovers. They were found in bed.

Vera And PROSPER?

Kieffer DENISE and ARCHAMBAUD had been forging identity cards in their flat. On the table was the one theywere making for this man. [*Pointing to the photograph in* **Vera***'s hand*] Desprez . . . François Desprez. Not his real name of course. But we had his address. Watched his flat for hours. Then he walked in. We would never have caught him otherwise.

Vera He's brought to Avenue Foch . . .

Kieffer Brought to Avenue Foch, where his friends already were. Had them all on the top floor in separate rooms. Vogt translated. [*Laughing*] Thought they were all French. After a while I could do it myself as we found they all spoke English.

Vera PROSPER?

Kieffer He was very brave.

Vera Did he talk?

Kieffer No.

Vera No?

Kieffer Not at first. [*Pause*] He was mad . . . cocky. Refused *everything* offered to him. [*Stubbing out his cigarette*] Except cigarettes. They couldn't resist my English cigarettes. [*He smiles*]

Vera He *did* talk then?

Kieffer PROSPER . . . in the end realised he was in a difficult, impossible situation. As did ARCHAMBAUD, who crumbled very swiftly . . . and all of them.

Vera And why was that?

Kieffer The evidence we were able to present. Most were made to feel they had nothing to lose because we knew so much already. First to PROSPER . . .

Vera Aside from the fact you broke his arm and beat him senseless.

Kieffer I am not aware of this . . .

Vera The F Section had no traitors then? There was no one who willingly betrayed us?

Kieffer You are asking me if there was a traitor in your ranks? But why are you asking me? You know yourself there was one. You recalled him to London . . . GILBERT. He was Karl Boemelburg's agent. More than an agent in fact, he was a friend to him, going back a very long time. Boemelburg alone dealt with him. [*Pause*] He had a symbol. [*Grabs the pen on his desk and writes*] B . . . O . . . E . . . *achtundvierzig.* Boemelburg's forty-eighth agent. His 'super ace.'

Vera And who exactly was BOE 48?

Kieffer [*looking puzzled*] Well, I think you know. Of course you know. It was Henri Déricourt.

Vera What evidence . . . were you able to present to our agents?

Kieffer Evidence gathered from two key sources.

Vera Which were?

Kieffer Déricourt . . .

Vera Who was arranging many of our planes, receptions and drops. And collecting our agents' mail.

Kieffer Yes, the mail was extremely useful. Not at first. We photographed it and put it in the safe, but we didn't put much store by it when it was first presented it to us. Once we had PROSPER, Boemelburg passed the copies of PROSPER's letters to me and I handed them to August Scherer.

Vera Did Scherer carry out PROSPER's interrogation?

Kieffer Yes. I remember Scherer was very happy to have all this material to use and PROSPER was astonished that we knew this and that.

Vera And then PROSPER talked?

Kieffer PROSPER did not wish to make a full statement, but this was not the case with ARCHAMBAUD who had not the integrity of PROSPER and made a very full statement.

Vera You made a pact then? Lives saved for information?

Kieffer If a deal was done it was arranged and agreed by Horst Kopkow in Berlin. All I can tell you is that your agents were treated very well at Avenue Foch.

Vera What was the other source of evidence?

Kieffer You know this too.

Vera Do I?

Kieffer You were playing it as well.

Vera You'll have to enlighten me . . .

Kieffer *Funkspiel?* The radio game? You'll already have interviewed Goetz.

Vera I am here to know your take on it.

Kieffer Well *our* game began with VALENTIN and BERTRAND, two Canadians we picked from your ARCHDEACON Circuit. But then it was ARCHAMBAUD's radio . . . BUTCHER. Found under a lettuce at Le Collège National de L'Ecole d'Agriculture at Grignon. Although I believe the game has also been very successfully played elsewhere.

Vera When did you start to play ARCHAMBAUD's radio back to us?

Kieffer Let's see. He came to us in late June. It would only have taken Goetz a few days to be able to emulate ARCHAMBAUD's [*tapping the desk as if using Morse code,* **Kieffer** *then makes a fist*] *Faust.*

Vera Fist.

Kieffer Goetz was exceptionally skilled. He was able to play back BUTCHER's radio in July '43. It wasn't perfect, it had the false check, but not the true check. In the end it did not matter, as London did not seem to mind terribly. [*Pauses to recollect*] I can still remember ARCHAMBAUD's face when he learned his message had got through and been accepted. He was white, white as a sheet. I mean . . . the colour . . . just drained from him. Then after that there was NURSE or DIANA . . . Goetz's own name for it.

[*At this point* **Vera** *shows* **Kieffer** *a photograph of* **Noor**. *At the same moment* **Noor** *appears and stands at the edge of the room/ perimeter of the stage, she might appear and move through the audience and take a seat on the front row*]

Enter **Noor**

Kieffer MADELEINE. There she is.

Vera When did *her* game commence?

Kieffer MADELEINE was brought to us in October '43.

Vera *October?*

Kieffer Yes. We started fairly soon after her arrival which is why I imagine you continued to believe she was still at large for so long after her capture. By November, Goetz said he didn't need her to work her radio. It was simple to impersonate her because our signals staff had been listening into her traffic for such a long time. He also had a notebook in his possession taken from MADELEINE'S flat.

Vera Containing what?

Kieffer All her back messages, very neatly written out. From this we could work out her code and all her security checks.

[*Dismayed,* **Vera** *puts her head in her hands*]

Kieffer MADELEINE was quite something though. Didn't know what to do with her. She never complied. She told us nothing.

Vera [*quietly to herself*] She found a way . . . like the King of Benares.

Kieffer What do you mean?

Vera *Whosoever talks beyond measure comes by some misery of this kind. And thenceforward the King abstained from talking and became a man of few words.*

Kieffer We could not rely on anything she said. I cannot remember her real name but I am sure in this she also lied to us.

Vera [*curtly*] She wouldn't have lied. [*Beat*] She was known to us Nora Baker, but her real name was Noor Inayat Khan. Father was a Sufi leader. She had connections with Indian royalty.

Kieffer A spy . . . princess. [*Pause*] Vogt spent hours with her. Offered her everything. English tea, biscuits. She refused it all. Absolutely maddening. She could be heard though, crying in her room at night, telling stories to herself.

Vera She was a children's author.

Kieffer And this . . . was a suitable person to send to war?

Vera Our agents came from many walks of life. [*Pause*] Where was she sent in November?

Kieffer MADELEINE went to prison in Karlsruhe. We sent other women there too.

Vera Why did you send her away?

Kieffer I told you she was no longer needed. We had captured so many I was running out of room!

Vera A victim of your own success?

Kieffer I'm sorry but I simply couldn't take the risk anymore, not after she tried to escape.

Vera From the roof? After a bath?

Kieffer That was only the first. The second was more calculated in its execution and involved others.

Vera Who?

Kieffer Bob Starr and Lionel Faye. [*Pause*] One night at about three in the morning I was awakened in my room by the guard to say Bob and MADELEINE had escaped. They, with the French resistance leader, Colonel Faye had broken through the iron bars in the cells leading to the window of the ceiling and they climbed onto the flat roof. By means of sheets and blankets, knotted together, they let themselves down on to the balcony on the third storey of a neighbouring house and there smashed a window and entered the apartment. Had they not been recaptured it is assumed that all the radio plays which were in full swing would have been finished.

Vera That would have been devastating.

Kieffer Damn right!

Vera Bob Starr has told us you lined them up against the wall on the fourth floor to be shot.

Kieffer I was mad as hell! So . . . disappointed with them! How could they do that when we had treated them so well? I sent them back to their rooms, I couldn't even look at them. In the morning I insisted that the three give me their word of honour, not to attempt to escape again. Only Bob agreed. He stayed, I couldn't keep the other two anymore.

Vera And off went MADELEINE to chains, low rations, beatings and eventually . . . death! [*Angrily*] *Die Genfer Konvention besagt . . .*

Kieffer [*suddenly, matching her anger*] The Geneva Convention, Squadron Officer, does not apply here. As well you know. These are not soldiers. They're spies. In civilian clothes. They have no rank. They have no status!

Vera And this is an important distinction for you, isn't it Kieffer? One could say your life depends on it. [*Noting his alarm*] Don't worry, I will leave SAS matters for Major Barkworth. My concern here is to discuss F Section.

[**Noor** *stands from where she has been seated or moves from the shadows at the perimeter of the stage. It is now clear she is dressed in the WAAF uniform* **Vera** *had in the parcel in Scene Two*]

Kieffer At the end of the day, I am a policeman . . . policing is my interest, my profession . . . not punishments.

[**Vera** *now sees* **Noor** *for the first time in* **Kieffer***'s cell. There is moment between the women and then* **Vera** *nods to* **Noor**]

Vera But you are . . . Gestapo?

Kieffer Of course.

Vera And every member of the Gestapo will be familiar with the *Nacht und Nebel Aktion* . . . night and fog? Kieffer, I have spent the last eighteen months of my life tracing any scrap of evidence left of twelve of our missing female agents. It has been a near impossible task. You have left us so little to go on, we've almost had to summon the dead to give us a clue.

[**Noor** *begins to fade back into the shadows until she is no longer visible*]

[*Exit* **Noor**

Kieffer Such nonsense . . .

Vera [*bitterly*] MADELEINE was very valuable to you, wasn't she? I understand you paid a lot of money to the woman who betrayed her? I'm sure you'd be interested to know what happened to her after she left Pforzheim Prison? Of course you know at Pforzheim she was chained hand to foot to her bed in such a way that she could never stand straight. She was in isolation, she was starved. You'll know this because you sent her there. You know this because you requested it. The restraints were your idea.

Kieffer MADELEINE was considered a dangerous prisoner because of her escapes. If she had escaped again she certainly would have been shot. Most Gestapo officers would have shot her after her first attempt.

Vera She remained at Pforzheim in those conditions for ten months. On 12th September she was put on a train and taken with three of our other women to Dachau Concentration Camp. [**Kieffer** *suddenly looks up, surprised*] Now it's been hard to piece together all the details, but shortly after they arrived at Dachau they were all executed. MADELEINE . . . *Noor* . . . because of the colour of skin was singled out for special treatment by some thug – who is unimportant – and who was probably cleared up and hung by the trials we've already had. Noor was beaten all night long, I dare say raped, and shot in the early hours of the thirteenth. All four women were fed to the furnace.

[**Kieffer** *begins to cry.* **Vera** *allows this for a few moments but then puts a stop to it*]

Vera Kieffer, if one of us is going to cry it is going to be me. You will stop this comedy. I will a draw up a short deposition of what of we have discussed today for you to sign.

[**Kieffer** *nods, wiping his eyes with his handkerchief.* **Vera** *gestures to the photograph on his desk*]

Vera *Ist das Ihre Tochter?*

Kieffer *Ja. Hildegard. Sie ist neunzehn. Meine Jüngste.* She came over to stay with me at Christmas. Major Barkworth and the English officers. It was quite a party. [*Turns to look out of his window*] *Kiebitz.* Funny little bird with the . . . [*Gesturing to the top of his own head to indicate the prominent feathers*] It's always there . . . must be cold.

Vera [*looking out of the window*] It's a lapwing.

Kieffer Now it's gone . . . [*Looking at* **Vera**] It's a good sign?

Vera [*looking him straight in the eye*] I have always thought so. [**Vera** *starts to pack her papers away*]

[**Kieffer** *continues to look out of the window*]

[*The beginning of Catherine Ribeiro's version of* Le Chant des Partisans *is played as lights fade to black*]

[*Three projected placards will appear with brief details of what happened to* **Kieffer**, **Vera** and **Noor**]

[Placard One: In August 1944 Hans Josef Kieffer received the order to shoot seven SAS prisoners. The execution of uniformed soldiers was contrary to the Geneva Convention. On 8th August, the SAS officers were dressed in civilian clothes and driven to a forest near Noailles and executed. It was the testimony of the two escapees which resulted in **Kieffer**'s trial and execution. He was executed by hanging at Hamelin prison by Albert Pierrepoint on 26th June 1947.]

[Placard Two: After the liberation of France, **Vera Atkins** was determined to uncover the fates of fifty-one, still unaccounted for, F Section agents. **Vera Atkins** not only uncovered how and where they died but by detailing their bravery before and after capture. She helped to ensure that each received official recognition by the British Government. Following **Kieffer**'s testimony, **Noor Inayat Khan** was posthumously awarded the George Cross in 1949.]

[Placard Three: Nothing, neither her nationality nor the traditions of her family obliged her **(Noor Inayat Khan)** to take her position in the war. However, she chose it. It is our fight that she chose, that she pursued with admirable and invincible courage. Madame de Gaulle-Anthonioz, the General's niece, President of l'Association Nationale des Anciennes Déportées et Internees de la Résistance.]

To all those who served and sacrificed for our freedom.
We will remember.
'Only the dark, dark night shows to our eyes the stars'

Walt Whitman

Le Chant des Partisans

Ami, entends-tu le vol noir des corbeaux sur nos plaines ?
Ami, entends-tu les cris sourds du pays qu'on enchaîne ?
Ohé, partisans, ouvriers et paysans, c'est l'alarme.
Ce soir l'ennemi connaîtra le prix du sang et les larmes.

Montez de la mine, descendez des collines, camarades !
Sortez de la paille les fusils, la mitraille, les grenades.
Ohé, les tueurs à la balle et au couteau, tuez vite !
Ohé, saboteur, attention à ton fardeau : dynamite . . .

C'est nous qui brisons les barreaux des prisons pour nos frères.
La haine à nos trousses et la faim qui nous pousse, la misère.

Il y a des pays où les gens au creux des lits font des rêves.
Ici, nous, vois-tu, nous on marche et nous on tue, nous on crève . . .

Ici chacun sait ce qu'il veut, ce qu'il fait quand il passe.
Ami, si tu tombes un ami sort de l'ombre à ta place.
Demain du sang noir sèchera au grand soleil sur les routes.
Chantez, compagnons, dans la nuit la Liberté nous écoute . . .

Ami, entends-tu ces cris sourds du pays qu'on enchaîne ?
Ami, entends-tu le vol noir des corbeaux sur nos plaines ?
Oh oh oh oh oh oh oh oh oh oh oh oh oh oh . . .

Scene Four (abridged)

[*Darkness*]

[**Vera Atkins**, *now nearly eighty years of age, is being interviewed for the Imperial War Museum Archive. She sits in a chair – lit from the front so she appears in silhouette – smoking a cigarette*]

[*Sound of a projection wheel and* Vera*'s voice from the Imperial War Museum sound archive recording (1987)*]

Vera Well, I was based with the legal section of War Crimes which was in Bad Oeynhausen, head of the British Army on the Rhine . . . and I worked from there. I was only interested in tracing . . . the people who had gone to concentration camps and who had not returned and to find out how and where they were killed and I assisted the prosecution in three war crimes trials.

[*Projection of a placard: January 1947, Allied Occupied Germany*]

[*Sound of the inside of a prison. Mens' voices, prison officers shouting orders, doors locking and unlocking*]

Lights up on **Vera** *and* **Kieffer**

[**Kieffer** *is dressed in civilian clothes*]

Vera Well . . . I would like to begin with asking you about the capture of three of our agents starting from June '43. [*Still rummaging through her briefcase*]

Kieffer June '43.

Vera Yes.

Kieffer The agents?

Vera [*taking a file from a briefcase, opening it and holding out a photograph to* **Kieffer**]

Kieffer MADELEINE. There she is.

Vera She was known to us Nora Baker, but her real name was Noor Inayat Khan.

Kieffer MADELEINE went to prison in Karlsruhe. We sent other women there too.

Vera Why did you send her away?

Kieffer I'm sorry but I simply couldn't take the risk anymore, not after she tried to escape.

Vera And off went MADELEINE to chains, low rations, beatings and eventually . . . death! [*Angrily*] *Die Genfer Konvention besagt . . .*

Kieffer [*suddenly, matching her anger*] The Geneva Convention, Squadron Officer, does not apply here. As well you know. These are not soldiers. They're spies. In civilian clothes. They have no rank. They have no status! At the end of the day, I am a policeman . . . policing is my interest, my profession . . . not punishments.

Vera But you are . . . Gestapo?

Kieffer Of course.

Vera And every member of the Gestapo will be familiar with the *Nacht und Nebel Aktion* . . . night and fog? Kieffer, I have spent the last eighteen months of my life tracing any scrap of evidence left of twelve of our missing female agents. It has been a near impossible task. You have left us so little to go on. We've almost had to summon the dead to give us a clue.

Kieffer Such nonsense . . .

Vera [*bitterly*] MADELEINE was very valuable to you, wasn't she? I understand you paid a lot of money to the woman who betrayed her? I'm sure you'd be interested to know what happened to her after she left Pforzheim Prison? Of course, you know at Pforzheim she was chained hand to foot to her bed in such a way that she could never stand straight. She was in isolation, she was starved. You'll know this because you sent her there. You know this because you requested it. The restraints were your idea.

Kieffer MADELEINE was considered a dangerous prisoner because of her escapes. If she had escaped again she certainly would have been shot. Most Gestapo officers would have shot her after her first attempt.

Vera She remained at Pforzheim in those conditions for ten months. On 12th September she was put on a train and taken with three of our other women to Dachau Concentration Camp. [**Kieffer** *suddenly looks up, surprised*] Now it's been hard to piece together all the details, but shortly after they arrived at Dachau they were all executed. MADELEINE . . . *Noor* . . . because of the colour of her skin was singled out for special treatment by some thug – who is unimportant – and who was probably cleared up and hung by the trials we've already had. Noor was beaten all night long, I dare say raped, and shot in the early hours of the thirteenth. All four women were fed to the furnace.

[**Kieffer** *begins to cry.* **Vera** *allows this for a few moments, but then puts a stop to it*]

Vera Kieffer, you will stop this comedy . . . if one of us is going to cry it is going to be me. [*She doesn't cry, but repeats*] It will be me.

[**Kieffer** *continues to look downward and does not raise his eyes as the lights fade*]

To all those who served and sacrificed for our freedom.

We will remember.

'Only the dark, dark night shows to our eyes the stars'

Walt Whitman

Le Chant des Partisans

Ami, entends-tu le vol noir des corbeaux sur nos plaines ?
Ami, entends-tu les cris sourds du pays qu'on enchaîne ?
Ohé, partisans, ouvriers et paysans, c'est l'alarme.
Ce soir l'ennemi connaîtra le prix du sang et les larmes.

Montez de la mine, descendez des collines, camarades !
Sortez de la paille les fusils, la mitraille, les grenades.
Ohé, les tueurs à la balle et au couteau, tuez vite !
Ohé, saboteur, attention à ton fardeau : dynamite...

C'est nous qui brisons les barreaux des prisons pour nos frères.
La haine à nos trousses et la faim qui nous pousse, la misère.
Il y a des pays où les gens au creux des lits font des rêves.
Ici, nous, vois-tu, nous on marche et nous on tue, nous on crève...

Ici chacun sait ce qu'il veut, ce qu'il fait quand il passe.
Ami, si tu tombes un ami sort de l'ombre à ta place.
Demain du sang noir sèchera au grand soleil sur les routes.

Chantez, compagnons, dans la nuit la Liberté nous écoute...
Ami, entends-tu ces cris sourds du pays qu'on enchaîne ?
Ami, entends-tu le vol noir des corbeaux sur nos plaines ?
Oh oh oh oh oh oh oh oh oh oh oh oh oh oh oh oh....

Memories

Zenna Hopson's memories of Vera Atkins

Vera Atkins was my remarkable Aunt. As this play will show she became well known for her work in S.O.E preparing agents to go behind enemy lines. She is well known for relentless identifying what happened to the 117 female agents she behind enemy lines, after the war. She is even well known for her work in establishing the first French UK school exchanges in her passion for a peaceful united Europe. However, she is best known to me as my Aunt Vera, the woman who washed my hands before meals, let me play with her abundant crazy ornaments, who look me to feed the ducks on Hyde Park Pond. The woman who as I got older, smoked without inhaling, never left my wine glass empty for long and who could cook a three-course meal out of leftovers. She was brilliant, challenging, fun and fascinating. She was my Aunt Vera.

Sandy Guthrie's memories of his father Captain Duncan Dunbar Guthrie, OBE

Duncan Guthrie's involvement with SOE was as a member of one of the Jedburgh teams. Unlike agents who were sent to France dressed as civilians, the Jeds were in uniform, helping the resistance on the ground with sabotage and guerrilla warfare – the uniforms demonstrating that support was available.

Each team comprised a British or American officer, an officer from the country in question (in this case France) and a radio operator. Team Harry, with a French officer, a French radio operator plus Duncan, was dropped into France on June 6th, 1944 – D Day – in the Morvan region, 150 miles south east of Paris.

Simon Rymills' memories of his father S.O.E. Pilot, Flying Officer F.E. Bunny Rymills, DFC & Bar, DFM

Memories from my father during a journey across France, May 1982. I had been asked to drive, he said he felt a lot safer in the air 'dodging the German air defences rather than dodging the French drivers! My father had been invited by the French Government to the opening of La Musée Départemental de la Résistance Henri Quielle by François Mitterrand and Jacques Chirac. During the journey he talked about the landing fields and the agents he had met during this time. One SOE agent in particular was Noor Inayat Khan. I asked my father what sort of person she was, and he replied: 'a gentle and quietly spoken woman, not really suited to warfare.' They met on several occasions out of the moon period, when agents were introduced to the pilots and discussed the flight, embarkation, and the reception party on the ground. Noor spoke to Dad several times; she had a very reserved manner with some apprehension about the impending sortie. He took her aside to quell her anxiety and told her that he would talk to her again during the flight via the intercom to put her at ease. I believe Noor was thankful to Dad for these kind thoughts. The night of the operation went well. Dad took off and followed as second aircraft. Noor was wearing a green oil skin coat, dark trousers, and a beret. He recollected that she looked quite comical and 'not too hot.' Later during our journey Dad told me how upset he had been when the news broke of her execution in Dachau. He was devastated to hear that such a gentle and talented woman had been killed by a bunch of murderous thugs. 'But the SD Gestapo hadn't obtained any information from her. She was one of the bravest women I've ever met without doubt.'

Dad retired from the RAF in August 1963 after some twenty-five years, and in twenty-one years of flying aircraft, I don't think he ever forgot Noor Inayat Khan KGC.

BEST BELOVED

Best Beloved is based on the true story of Rudyard Kipling's near fatal visit to America in 1899. From the outset nothing went according to plan as the whole family was struck down by illness. Kipling and his eldest daughter, Josephine, suffered the most serious cases.

The story is told by an outsider – a young stenographer called Martha Pitcher – who is employed to record the writer's fevered dreams. The action moves between the chaos of the media throng surrounding the Kiplings' Manhattan hotel and from within one of Kipling's hallucinations (where he imagines he's trapped inside a whale).

Tragically, as Kipling begins to show signs of recovery, Josephine dies. Kipling's doctors recommend that he is not made aware of the loss for fear of jeopardizing his health.

In 1902, three years after Josephine's death, Kipling would publish the *Just So Stories* in her memory. His dreams are archived at the University of Sussex.

Best Beloved

by

Deborah Clair

To my father and to my mother
Tom and Pat Morris

Characters

Rudyard Kipling (1865–1936)	English author in his thirties (speaks with a polished English accent)
Caroline 'Carrie' Kipling (1862–1939)	Rudyard's wife in her thirties (speaks with a New England accent)
Josephine Kipling / The Stute Fish (1892–99)	Rudyard and Caroline's seven year old daughter
Josephine Dunham (1870–1939)	Caroline's sister, in her late twenties (speaks with a New England accent)
Anna Balestier (1838–1919)	Caroline's mother, in her sixties (speaks with a New England accent)
Dr. Edward Janeway (1841–1911)	a lung specialist, in his fifties (speaks with a New England accent)
Dr. James Conland (1851–1903)	family doctor, in his forties (speaks with a New England accent)
Rudolph Block (1870–1940)	a reporter, in his late twenties, from the New York World
Martha Pitcher	a young stenographer, eighteen years of age (speaks with a New England accent)
Frank Doubleday (1862–1934)	an American publisher in his thirties
Hotel Manager	(speaks with a New York accent)
Police Officer Delaney	(speaks with a New York accent)

Cast

Martha Pitcher / Anna Balestier	Deborah Clair
Rudyard Kipling / Police Officer Delaney	Tim Marriott
Dr. James Conland / Rudolph Block	Daniel Bennett
Dr. Janeway / Frank Doubleday / Hotel Manager	Nicholas Collett
Caroline 'Carrie' Kipling	Lucy Dent
Josephine Dunham	Niamh Bennett
Josephine Kipling / The Stute Fish	Esme Bennett

Best Beloved was written and recorded as a radio drama in 2020.

Produced by Nicholas Collett

Best Beloved was a CLAIR/OBSCUR production hosted by Smokescreen Productions

A note on the staging

The playscript printed here has been devised for a staged performance. If ***Best Beloved*** is to be performed in its original form as a radio drama then the extracts from Martha Pitcher's diary can be performed as voiceovers/narration.

Scene One

[*Opening bars of Debussy's Clair de Lune (1913 recording)*]

[*Extract from* **Martha Pitcher** *'s Diary*]

Martha Pitcher [*centre stage in spotlight, holding her travelling typewriter case, speaking with a slightly dream-like quality*]

In the depth of your hopes and desires lies your silent knowledge of the beyond;

And like seeds dreaming beneath the snow your heart dreams of spring.

Trust the dreams, for in them is hidden the gate to eternity.

Khalil Gibran

[*Blackout*

Scene Two

[*1899*] [*The inside of a whale*]

[*Cool blue lighting, sound of being within an expansive chamber. Water dripping*]

[**Rudyard Kipling** *is wearing a night cap and in his dressing gown*]

Rudyard Kipling [*lying on the ground in a contorted position and slowly regaining consciousness*] Wat . . . er . . . dripping. Damp. Very damp. *Warm* . . . though. Not entirely unpleasant. [*Sits up with some effort*] Cavernous. Cavern . . . cave. [*Shouts*] HALLO! I say . . . HALLO!

[*His shout echoes and then silence*] Light . . . matches . . . pocket . . . [*Fumbles in pocket, finds matches, strikes match*] Quite extraordinary!

[*Lights fade, on* **Rudyard Kipling**]

Scene Three

[*New York, February 1899 – The Grenoble Hotel –* **Rudyard Kipling** *'s bedroom*]

[*Warm lights up on* **Dr. Janeway** *and* **Dr. Conland**]

Rudyard Kipling [*delirious, moaning and crying from the opposite side of the room*] Extra . . . or . . . dinary!

Dr. Janeway [*speaking softly*] Both lungs are known to be involved . . .

Dr. Conland Fever?

Dr. Janeway Runs high, delirium is . . . frequent. Both lungs are solidified, leaving scant space for inhalation and therefore . . .

[*Lights up on* **Martha Pitcher**, *as she types quickly*]

Dr. Janeway . . . preventing . . . [*Notices* **Martha Pitcher** *in the corner with her typewriter*] I'm sorry, what business has that girl being here?

Dr. Conland [*awkwardly acknowledging* **Martha** *'s presence*] I know. A long story. It's . . . permitted. A . . . er . . . 'request' from the patient.

Dr. Janeway [*continuing to recite symptoms*] . . . preventing the oxidization of the blood in the natural process . . .

Dr. Conland He's drowning. [*Beat*] Wright says . . .

Dr. Janeway I know. [*Beat*] But we must continue . . .

Dr. Conland You'll return later?

Dr. Janeway I shall. [*Putting his winter coat on*] What about the wife?

Dr. Conland I'm not sure how much she . . . [*Considers*] She's robust.

Dr. Janeway Free use of oxygen is necessary. We must try . . .

Dr. Conland Everything?

Dr. Janeway Everything . . . [*Opens the door to the corridor and goes to descend the stairs*] . . . else England will never forgive us! [**Dr. Janeway**'*s footsteps can be heard descending the stairs to the hotel lobby*]

[*Exit* **Dr. Janeway**

Scene Four

[*Extract from* **Martha Pitcher**'*s Diary*]

Martha Pitcher [*centre stage in spotlight*] England will never forgive us. That's certainly how it felt. The Kiplings had been entrusted to us Americans that winter of 1899. They were 'on loan' . . . 'handle with care.' [*Beat*] They were famous . . . world-famous. The most curious folk I've ever met and believe me I've met some crackpots. *He* was Rudyard Kipling . . . the most highly-regarded British writer of a generation, author of stories of the Empire and the Jungle Books. *She* was Caroline Kipling, a wealthy American from Vermont, guarded and steely. But this story is my story. How I, Martha Pitcher, a young girl, eighteen years old, found herself . . . *swallowed whole* . . . into the chaos of the Kiplings' world, if only to be spat out a few weeks later. There had already been much speculation in the press about the purpose of the Kiplings' visit. I guess folks still remembered the drama of when they'd tried to make America their home. Family disputes made painfully public had driven them away. When they docked in New York with their three young children on a cold February morning, there was the usual throng of reporters and well-wishers trailing them all the way to the Grenoble Hotel on West 56th Street.

[*Blackout*

Scene Five

[*The Grenoble Hotel's lobby – filled with people – mostly reporters. Sound of photographs being taken, lots of commotion, excitement, toddlers crying and children coughing*]

Enter **Rudyard Kipling, Caroline Kipling** *with their children and the* **Hotel Manager**

Hotel Manager This way Mrs. Kipling, let's get you installed in your rooms. I gather you've had a terribly trying journey. [*Calls to* **Bell Boy**] Luke, please supervise the transfer of Mr. and Mrs. Kipling's baggage to the third floor! [*To* **Police Officer**] Officer, can you get rid of these people?

Police Officer [*shouting*] OK folks, time to wrap it up now! You've had your fun. Move towards the door please . . . [*The noise of the press and photographers fades into the background*]

Enter **Anna Balestier** *and* **Josephine Dunham**

Anna Balestier Caroline . . . dearest!

Caroline Kipling Mother, how I've missed you all!

Josephine Dunham Carrie . . . Theo managed to listen to the girls' chests on our way over in the cab. He thinks it might be whooping cough . . .

Anna Balestier Whooping cough! Oh my dear!

Enter **Rudolph Block**

Rudolph Block Mr. Kipling . . . Sir! Rudolph Block, the New York Times. We met a couple of years ago. May I ask what brings you back to New York?

Rudyard Kipling You may *ask*, Mr. Block, but I have absolutely nothing to say.

Anna Balestier [*running through her own checklist of remedies*] Rest . . . no exertion permitted whatsoever for these little darlings. [*To* **Hotel Manager**] Excuse me. Might I ask you to request the head chef prepare some soup . . .

Hotel Manager Of course, ma'am.

Anna Balestier . . . for my grand-daughters.

Josephine Dunham Any fluids will do mother . . .

Anna Balestier I can . . . dictate or write down the recipe for this. [*Rummaging in her handbag*] Where are my eyeglasses? [*Finds her eyeglasses*] Ah! Now . . . does anyone have pencil and paper?

Hotel Manager Luke will be able to locate paper and pencils in your daughter's room, ma'am.

Josephine Dunham [*trying to move her mother* **Anna** *along*] Yes, in Carrie's room mother. Look, there's an elevator.

Anna Balestier [*getting into the elevator*] Honestly Caroline, a winter crossing . . . what possessed you?

Caroline Kipling You go ahead mother with the girls. Ruddy and I will follow with Johnny.

[*Exit* **Anna Balestier** *and* **Josephine Dunham**

[*Sound of elevator doors closing and the lift ascending*

Rudyard Kipling [*hanging back*] Carrie, I'm just giving . . . Mr. Block is it . . . ?

Rudolph Block [*re-introducing himself*] Rudolph Block Sir, Ma'am.

Rudyard Kipling Five minutes of my time and then I'll be up directly.

Caroline Kipling Ruddy, you don't look well yourself. Please don't be long.

Rudyard Kipling [*softly to* **Caroline**] Feed the wolves an early breakfast then they'll leave us alone 'til dinner. [*Loudly*] Five minute and then I'll be sprinting up the stairs.

Caroline Kipling Absolutely no sprinting. [*Taking her leave*] Mr. Block.

[*Sound of elevator door opening*]

[*Exit* **Caroline** *stepping in to the elevator*

Rudolph Block Mrs. Kipling. My best wishes to the children for a strong recovery.

[*Sound of elevator door closing and the lift ascending*

Rudyard Kipling All right Mr. Block. Five minutes on the purpose of my visit to your great country . . .

Rudolph Block *Our* great country Sir, surely?

Rudyard Kipling Ha! That it is Mr. Block, that it is! It's good to be back.

Rudolph Block We'll not be disturbed in here Sir.

[*Exit* **Block** and **Kipling** as **Block** *shows* **Kipling** *into a private lounge*

[*The sound of the crowd fades*

Scene Six

[*1899*] [*The inside a whale*]

[*Sound of being within an expansive chamber. Water dripping*]

[**Rudyard Kipling** *is SC. He is wearing a night cap and in his dressing gown. He is briefly visible as he strikes each match*]

Rudyard Kipling [*lighting another match to illuminate his surroundings*] An undiscovered country? [*Match goes out. He lights another*] Puzzles the will. [*Match goes out. He lights another*] What's that? Little rock pool? [*Match burns out. He lights another*] Yeeees . . . it is! [*Drawing nearer*] Ahhh . . . damn! [*The match burns his finger*]

[*Thunderous sound of a whale from the inside. Sound of* **Kipling** *splashing into the water with this sudden blast*]

Scene Seven

[*Extract from* **Martha Pitcher***'s diary*]

Martha Pitcher [*aside*] The Kiplings had three children. Golden-haired Josephine was the first and, without doubt, Kipling's favourite. Best beloved . . . Bo.

[*Blackout*

Scene Eight

[**Josephine Kipling***'s bedroom, Sussex, England, 1897*]

[*Fade up on dream-like sounds of laughter as a little girl – six years of age – is being chased around her bedroom by her father*]

Enter **Josephine Kipling** *and* **Rudyard Kipling**

Rudyard Kipling Such a naughty cub! What are we to do with her? Put her in the tower . . . ? [**Josephine** *laughs*] Throw her in the dungeon . . . ? [**Josephine** *shrieks*] Cast her out to sea? [**Josephine** *screams*] [**Kipling** *pretends to be a sea captain*] Yes, I think there's we have it!

Caroline Kipling [*offstage, calling*] Ruddy! Ruddy . . . this is too noisy a game for bedtime. Bo will never get to sleep . . .

Rudyard Kipling [*calling to* **Caroline**] Of course my dearest. [*Suddenly serious*] Into bed now Bo.

Josephine Kipling But I'm not sleepy. I'm going to America! [*Sound of bedsprings as* **Josephine** *bounces on her bed*]

Rudyard Kipling I'm excited too Bo but we heard what mother said didn't we? [*Beat*] Didn't we?

Josephine Kipling We did. [*Beat*] But I'd go to sleep quicker . . . with a story.

Rudyard Kipling Hmmm . . . [*Becoming the sea captain again*] Then this I propose: a tale of the sea in return for a little girl washed, combed and ready for bed five minutes after. Do we have an accord missy?

Josephine Kipling Have an accord!

Rudyard Kipling Very well. What'll it be? The whale! The whale . . . indeed! Very well! [*Clearing throat theatrically*] On the sea, once upon a time, O my Best Beloved, there was a whale and he ate fishes.

Josephine Kipling [*reciting by heart*] He ate the starfish and the garfish, and the crab and the dab, and the plaice and the dace, and the skate and his mate, and the mackereel and the pickereel and the really truly twirly-whirly eel . . .

Rudyard Kipling All the fishes he could find in all the sea he ate with his mouth . . . so! [*Making eating noises*] Till at last there was only one small fish in all the sea and he was a small Stute Fish. [*To* **Josephine**] That's you Bo . . . and he swam a little behind the whale's right ear so as to be out of harm's way. Then the whale stood on his tail . . .

Josephine Kipling Can they do that?

Rudyard Kipling Oh yes they can. [*Resuming*] Then the whale stood on his tail and said 'I'm hungry.' They do it especially when they're hungry. [*Resuming*] And the small Stute Fish said in a small stute voice . . . [*To* **Josephine**] Can you remember?

Josephine Kipling 'Noble and . . . '

Rudyard Kipling ' . . . generous Cetaccean, have you ever tasted Man?' [*Praising her*] Very good. 'No' said the whale. 'What is it like?'

Josephine Kipling 'Nice.'

Rudyard Kipling Said the small stute fish. 'Nice . . . but nubbly.' [*Giggling*] 'Then fetch me some.'

Josephine Kipling The stute fish said 'If you swim to latitude Fifty North, longitude Forty West (that is Magic) you will find sitting on a raft in the middle of the sea, with nothing on but a pair of blue canvas breeches, a pair of suspenders . . . '

Rudyard Kipling You must not forget the suspenders, Best Beloved.

Josephine Kipling . . . and a jack knife, one shipwrecked Mariner . . .

Rudyard Kipling ' . . . who, it is only fair to tell you, is a man of infinite resource and sagacity.' So the whale swam and swam to a latitude Fifty North, longitude Forty West . . .

[*Slow fade on* **Kipling***'s voice*

Scene Nine

[*Extract from* **Martha Pitcher***'s diary*]

Martha Pitcher [*aside*] It was mere luck that the call came to me. I was a typist at Doubleday and McClure, a new publisher on Broadway. An urgent cable arrived: Stenographer requested for Mr. Rudyard Kipling, Grenoble Hotel, West 56th. Mr. Doubleday, my boss, was already there in attendance. In fact, he had been for the best part of two weeks. I guess he really wanted this new client. When I arrived at the Grenoble – with my typewriter – I was sent straight up to the third floor. It was a stricken Mrs. Kipling who opened the door.

[*Blackout*

Scene Ten

[*New York, February 1899 – The Grenoble Hotel – corridor outside* **Rudyard Kipling***'s bedroom*]

Caroline Kipling [*opening the door*] Yes?

Enter **Martha Pitcher**

Martha Pitcher Good morning Ma'am. My name is Martha Pitcher . . .

Caroline Kipling Yes?

Martha Pitcher I was sent by my employers . . .

Caroline Kipling I'm afraid this is a mistake . . . we've made no . . .

Martha Pitcher . . . Doubleday and McClure . . .

Caroline Kipling . . . request for . . . I'm sorry . . . Doubleday? *Effendi*?

Martha Pitcher Effendi? I'm . . . I'm sorry . . .

Enter **Frank Doubleday**

Frank Doubleday Carrie, this is my doing!

Martha Pitcher [*aside*] Frank Nelson Doubleday. Brooklyn born, clawed his way up in the printing business from the age of fourteen, but you'd never have guessed. Doubleday was as sharp and polished as his English-made shoes.

Frank Doubleday [*he approaches the door and sees* **Martha**] *Martha?* Was Daniel not available? Did Sam . . . er . . . Mr. McClure not get my wire?

Martha Pitcher Daniel . . . was delayed . . . the snowfall . . . um . . .

Frank Doubleday I see. [*Lowers his voice. To* **Caroline**] Martha appears to be Daniel's replacement. I'm not sure Sam has understood our needs . . .

Caroline Kipling I see.

Frank Doubleday Well . . . perhaps there is a way to make this work.

Caroline Kipling Frank . . . how?? She's a girl!!!

Martha Pitcher My typing speed is, in fact, faster than Daniel's, and my certificate is the higher . . .

Caroline Kipling Miss . . . ?

Martha Pitcher P . . . Pitcher.

Caroline Kipling Miss Pitcher, your qualifications are not in question here. This is *not* a regular typing job. My husband is . . . incapacitated, he is unwell . . . my daughter Josephine too. It's all . . . [*Sighing*] My husband is in bed and it would not be appropriate for a young girl such as yourself . . .

Martha Pitcher Oh, I understand.

Frank Doubleday [*to* **Caroline**] Let me make a telephone call . . .

Rudyard Kipling [*offstage, in a weak voice calling from his bed*] Effendi!

Frank Doubleday To see who else . . .

Rudyard Kipling [*offstage, calling with effort*] Eff-end-i!

Frank Doubleday . . . can be spared . . . yes? Here . . . Rud? [*Sound of footsteps as he retreats back in to* **Kipling***'s bedroom*]

[*Exit* **Frank Doubleday**

Rudyard Kipling [*offstage, faintly from inside his bedroom*] I don't mind.

Frank Doubleday [*offstage*] Rud, I think Carrie's right . . .

Rudyard Kipling [*offstage, speaking slowly, short of breath*] I don't mind. [*Beat*] I don't mind, that is . . . if the young lady doesn't.

Martha Pitcher [*aside in spotlight*] And so my time with the Kiplings began. Mrs. Kipling relented to my employment on the condition that Mr. Doubleday was always present, as chaperone, to protect both our honours, although as her daughter's condition deteriorated, she was needed elsewhere and it became harder for her to insist on this rule. I'd been there a full hour that first morning before I broached the subject of what it was I would be required to type.

Enter **Frank Doubleday**

Martha Pitcher [*to* **Frank Doubleday**] Mr. Doubleday does Mr. Kipling need help with his . . . *letters*?

Frank Doubleday Letters? Heavens no, Martha. Mrs. Kipling handles all Mr. Kipling's correspondence.

Martha Pitcher Then . . . umm . . . what exactly am I needed for?

Frank Doubleday Ha! Heavens! No one's told you?

Martha Pitcher [*aside in spotlight*] And *here* it was . . .

Frank Doubleday [*lowering his voice, very serious*] Mr. Kipling is very interested – fascinated – in the unconscious mind. Since the onset of his pneumonia last week he has been experiencing delirium when his fever is high. Mr. Kipling is very anxious that his words be recorded . . .

Martha Pitcher *Recorded?*

Frank Doubleday Uh, huh. Typed. Every word.

Martha Pitcher Wouldn't it be better for him to just focus on . . . *getting better?*

Frank Doubleday Oh, he is.

Martha Pitcher I just thought that . . .

Frank Doubleday You're not here to think Martha.

Martha Pitcher With Mr. Kipling being ill, he . . .

Frank Doubleday Just type. [*Tapping the table, he pretends to type*] Every word. [*Walking away*] Or we'll see if Daniel can't get through that snow . . .

[**Doubleday***'s footsteps can be heard walking back into* **Kipling***'s bedroom*]

[*Exit* **Frank Doubleday**

Frank Doubleday [*offstage*] That's all settled then, Rud . . .

Scene Eleven

[*New York, February 1899 – The Grenoble Hotel – corridor outside* **Rudyard Kipling***'s bedroom*]

[*Extract from* **Martha Pitcher***'s diary*]

Martha Pitcher [*aside in spotlight*] I'd never seen Doubleday be so obliging to a client. In the space of two weeks he'd made himself indispensable . . . opening the mail, nursing Kipling, even cooking his meals. No wonder Kipling had already awarded Doubleday a new pet name – Effendi – a play on his initials, the Turkish word for Master. I took a room just along the corridor of the third floor so my skills could be called upon at speed. As strange as my new job was I guess I was happy to be considered useful. I might have boasted to my colleagues but I was sworn to secrecy, captive in the hotel. It wasn't long until the alarm was raised, around noon the following day. Kipling had a fever of 102 and was rambling a novel. My typewriter poised with ink and paper, all I needed to do was run along the corridor but as I stepped out I almost ran into a stampede of hotel porters.

[*Blackout*

Scene Twelve

[*New York, February 1899 – The Grenoble Hotel – corridor outside* **Rudyard Kipling**'*s bedroom*]

[*Sound of two porters carrying a young child on a stretcher, softly moaning and crying*]

Enter **Hotel Manager** *and* **Dr. Conland**

Hotel Manager [*guiding the stretcher*] Clear the hall please!

Dr. Conland [*attending to his patient*] Steady gentlemen. *Very* delicate situation. Minimal movements . . .

Enter **Martha Pitcher**

Dr. Conland [*to* **Martha**] Afternoon Miss!

Hotel Manager [*checking the elevator as the doors open*] As I feared, the elevator will not take the whole party so we must take the stairs.

Martha Pitcher Good afternoon . . . Doctor. Is this . . . ? Josephine? This is Mr. Kipling's daughter. What is the emergency?

Dr. Conland And *you* are?

Martha Pitcher Martha Pitcher. I am in his employment . . . newly.

Dr. Conland Well Miss Pitcher, Mr. Kipling's daughter is to be moved from the hotel to another . . . location.

Martha Pitcher For treatment?

Dr. Conland For rest! Now, if you'll excuse me Miss Pitcher we are in haste!

Hotel Manager [*hurrying ahead*] Thankfully, we are only on Three. Remember boys, the bottom turn of the stairs. Very sharp . . . very sharp.

[*Exit* **Hotel Manager** and **Dr. Conland**

Enter **Caroline Kipling**

Caroline Kipling [*emerging from* **Kipling***'s bedroom*] Martha, there you are.

Martha Pitcher You're leaving?

Caroline Kipling [*under great strain*] To attend to my daughter. Dr. Janeway will be with my husband presently. Josephine goes to the care of a friend. I would I could do it myself, but . . . my hands are more than full. [*Taking her leave*] Miss Pitcher.

[*Exit* **Caroline Kipling** *hurrying away*

Scene Thirteen

[*Blackout*]

[*1899*] [*The inside of a whale*]

[*Sound of being within an expansive chamber. Water dripping*]

[**Rudyard Kipling** *is SC wearing a night cap and dressing gown*]

Rudyard Kipling [*fumbling with matches, tries to strike them*] Arggghh! None left!! [*Throwing the box away in anger*] Right. [*Tries to recall what he's seen by the light of the matches*] Bearings. Eight paces ahead . . . was the rock pool. No more than eight though. Don't want to end up *in* it again. [*Counting his paces as he moves forward*] One, two, three, four, five, six, seven, e . . . [*Nearly falls in but pulls back*] Seven then. Found the rock pool. [*He sits down with effort*] Now what?

The Stute Fish [**Josephine***'s voice but distant, ghostly*] I was hoping you'd tell me.

Rudyard Kipling [*leaping to his feet*] Who said that? Who's there?

The Stute Fish It . . . was . . . me.

Rudyard Kipling But, I can't see you, where are you?

The Stute Fish I'm over here . . . behind you.

Rudyard Kipling I thought I was alone down here . . . in this cave.

The Stute Fish You're not.

Rudyard Kipling Evidently.

The Stute Fish You're not.

Rudyard Kipling Because now there is you.

The Stute Fish You're not . . . in a cave . . .

Rudyard Kipling *Not* in a cave?

The Stute Fish Like a cave . . . very like a cave . . .

Rudyard Kipling But not a cave. [*Beat*] If not a cave . . . then what?

The Stute Fish A whale.

Rudyard Kipling A whale?!

[*Sound of* **Martha**'s *typing grows louder and then fades*

Scene Fourteen

[*Extract from* **Martha Pitcher**'s *diary*]

Martha Pitcher [*aside in spotlight*] For the best part of a week, Mrs. Kipling went back and forth between her daughter's and husband's bedsides. Kipling's health had declined and although I hadn't descended to the hotel lobby since my arrival, I would see the ripples of the news spilling out onto Seventh Avenue below my window. News people stalked the Manhattan streets in packs, hunting for their prey. As Kipling was soundly asleep my services were requested in the mail room on the other side of the building, but first I had to cross the jungle of the Grenoble's Reception . . .

[*Blackout*

Scene Fifteen

[*The Grenoble Hotel's lobby – crowded with people, mostly reporters and photographers including a group of reporters three-deep around the* **Hotel Manager** *and his reception desk. Sound of great commotion*]

Hotel Manager One at a time please gentlemen, one at a time! If any more of you tell me you have a reservation in an attempt to get past me, or my assistant, I will instruct Officer Delaney to make an arrest! Now, Dr. Janeway will be here to make an announcement about Mr. Kipling at *five* but until then I have *nothing further* for you . . . ! [*The commotion continues*]

Enter **Martha Pitcher**

Hotel Manager [*catching sight of* **Martha**] Ah, Miss Pitcher! I have a message. Please go . . . to the . . .

Martha Pitcher The Mail Room? Already got it.

Hotel Manager Can we clear a path here gentlemen? This way Miss Pitcher! Mr. Doubleday is waiting for you. *Nothing* gentlemen, *nothing* until *five*!

[*Noise recedes.* **Martha** *makes her way to the mail room. Sound of mail room door opening and closing. The room is full of letters for* **Rudyard Kipling**]

Frank Doubleday Martha . . . good! You'll be here on this side with letters. This mail sack first. I'm already here on cables . . . What I need from you is to . . . open . . . with the knife . . . and if the name is not at the top – as it should be – skip, skip to the name at the bottom and then call it out to me. We then have a grading system in piles of importance. Now that is *unless* the envelope betrays any of the contents . . . government stamps, royal crests . . .

Martha Pitcher *Royal crests*?

Frank Doubleday Uh, huh. Those straight to me.

Martha Pitcher Royal?

Frank Doubleday Yes Martha. Royal crests. [*Grandly*] We are on the brink, the . . . precipice of losing something great and . . . all over the world . . . the great and the good are waking up to this! *Understand?* Are *you* awake Martha?

Martha Pitcher I um . . .

Frank Doubleday Are you awake?

Martha Pitcher Yes, yes . . . I'm awake.

Frank Doubleday That mail sack. This knife.

Scene Sixteen

[*Extract from* **Martha Pitcher***'s Diary*]

Martha Pitcher [*aside in spotlight*] Kipling's dreams or hallucinations were fevered, terrifying, sometimes sexual, but only one scenario was repetitious. The whale. At first this dream was in the background but it came to the fore with a vengeance the morning after Josephine was moved from the Grenoble. I couldn't help feeling there was a connection between these events.

[*Blackout*

Scene Seventeen

[*Partial blackout*]

[*1899*] [*The inside of a whale*]

[*Sound of being within an expansive chamber. Water dripping*]

[**Rudyard Kipling** *is sitting on a rock SC in spotlight wearing a night cap and dressing gown*]

The Stute Fish [*speaking from the shadows*] You have it, don't you?

Rudyard Kipling Sorry I'm . . .

The Stute Fish You have it . . .

Rudyard Kipling Not sure I follow?

The Stute Fish The knife.

Rudyard Kipling The . . .

The Stute Fish The jack-knife

Rudyard Kipling I'm still adjusting to what . . . you've just told me . . .

The Stute Fish And what is that?

Rudyard Kipling That I'm . . . *in a whale.*

The Stute Fish Oh . . . that.

Rudyard Kipling If it's not too rude to ask . . .

The Stute Fish Go on . . .

Rudyard Kipling Who or what . . . are you?

The Stute Fish A friend.

Rudyard Kipling A friend. I'm glad. [*Fumbling in his pocket*] Ah, well, it seems I do have the knife.

The Stute Fish Good . . . but have you anything else?

Rudyard Kipling What . . . else . . . could there be?

The Stute Fish You're being silly.

Rudyard Kipling I didn't think I was.

The Stute Fish Well . . . you always used to tell me. Just so.

Rudyard Kipling I did?

The Stute Fish Not to forget . . . to *remember.*

Rudyard Kipling Sss . . . suspenders.

The Stute Fish Good . . .

Rudyard Kipling My head's pounding.

The Stute Fish What about . . . if I told you . . . who I am . . .

Rudyard Kipling I . . . just . . . wish I could . . .

The Stute Fish Keep going. How about if I tell you . . . I'm . . . the Stute Fish.

Rudyard Kipling You are?

The Stute Fish You *know* what to do.

Rudyard Kipling I can't . . . think!

The Stute Fish But you . . . are a man . . . of infinite resource . . . and sagacity.

Rudyard Kipling Infinite . . . sagacity! [*Beat*] Wait . . . wait . . . ha! I know! I know what to do! How to escape! [*He starts to sing a sea shanty and clap his hands*] Farewell and adieu to you Spanish ladies, farewell and adieu to you ladies of Spain! Sing with me fish! Come with me! Sing! [*Singing*] For we've received order, for to sail to old England . . .

The Stute Fish I can't.

Rudyard Kipling Nonsense . . . everyone can sing! [*Singing*] But we hope very soon we shall see you again.

The Stute Fish Come with you.

Rudyard Kipling [*not hearing, still singing*] We'll rant and we'll roar like true British sailors. We'll rant and we'll roar across the salt seas . . .

[**Kipling** *sings louder and louder and with more and more gusto. His voice reverberates around the whale's insides. Sound of huge crowd of sailors join in the shanty. Sounds of disgruntled whale and water pressure building. Finally, the sound of release as the whale blows its water in a deafening crescendo*]

Scene Eighteen

[*New York, February 1899 – The Grenoble Hotel –* **Rudyard Kipling** *'s bedroom*]

Martha Pitcher [*aside*] I must have fallen asleep at my typewriter in Kipling's room that morning. I could see by the clock on the mantel it was already 10. I was alarmed to see a dark figure standing at the foot of Kipling's bed. I almost screamed, but as she spoke it was not a ghost or an angel, but obviously Mrs. Kipling.

Enter **Caroline Kipling**

Caroline Kipling [*to her sleeping husband*] If you live . . . will you forgive me?

Martha Pitcher [*aside*] Mrs. Kipling believed I was asleep or perhaps she was unaware of my presence at all. Either way, this was a private moment. I thought to speak but didn't know what to say. A soft tap on the door made the decision for me . . .

Enter **Dr. Conland**

Dr. Conland Caroline . . .

Martha Pitcher [*aside*] It was Dr. Conland, the family doctor.

Dr. Conland Carrie? Come on, you know this isn't advised.

Caroline Kipling Yes?

Dr. Conland The cab's arrived. We must make haste.

Martha Pitcher [*aside*] Mrs. Kipling did not turn immediately.

Caroline Kipling Yes . . . quite so. [*Turning*] Martha . . . ?

Martha Pitcher [*aside*] Mrs. Kipling saw me now. She moved towards me with a new urgency. She whispered in my ear.

Caroline Kipling She's gone. You know this but *he* . . . must not. It will kill him. We go to Fresh Pond this morning . . .

Martha Pitcher [*aside*] And that was all she could say. As the pair departed, I could hear Dr. Conland reassuring Mrs. Kipling, not about the passing of her daughter but how Doubleday planned to handle the press speculation.

Dr. Conland [*to* **Caroline** *in a low voice*] Frank's making an announcement this morning. Which reminds me . . . [*raising his voice slightly*] . . . Miss Pitcher? Mr. Doubleday has an urgent typing task for you in the mail room.

Martha Pitcher [*aside*] The mail room. Where I seemed to be spending half my time. As I went down to Reception I allowed Mrs. Kipling's words to sink in. Little Josephine was dead. This would be devastating news for Kipling, who was believed to be getting better. If he awoke he would wish to follow her. When he awoke he would wish he hadn't. When I reached the mail room, Doubleday was once again knee-deep in post, head buried in a long letter, pages all over the table. The sentences seemed to flow over several sheets of paper. At every turn of the page, Doubleday winced and sighed.

[*Blackout*

Scene Nineteen

[*The Mail Room at the Grenoble Hotel*]

Frank Doubleday [*skim reading to himself*] 'Dearest Madam . . . I am writing to you at the earliest . . . forgive the tardiness of this latest . . . it was my primary objective to seize upon . . . '

Enter **Martha Pitcher**

Frank Doubleday [*gesturing to* **Martha**] Martha, sit, sit. [*Flapping the pages of the letter*] Henry James. Why use nine words when you can use eighty-nine. There's a novel here in itself. Ahhh, dear Lord, dear Lord . . . 'May I express, dear lady, my abject joy in hearing the news that dear Rudyard's health . . .' dear Lord, Martha . . . [*The pages fall onto the table*] He doesn't realize. [*Sighing*] He cannot know.

Martha Pitcher When did she . . . ?

Frank Doubleday Early yesterday morning. His best beloved. If the pneumonia doesn't kill him then . . .

Martha Pitcher I . . . don't know what to say.

Frank Doubleday Words are meaningless. [*He thumps the table*] Action is everything. Does that machine over there have ink?

Martha Pitcher [*checking*] Yes.

Frank Doubleday Good. Here goes: 'Mr. Kipling has had a splendid day . . . [**Martha** *types*] that is . . . a comfortable day. He is beginning to take nourishment of a more substantial kind. Of course, he has the appearance of a man who has been at the point of death and his mind works very slowly. He has not been told of his daughter, Josephine's death.' New paragraph. 'It is Mrs. Kipling's earnest wish that all matters connected with the funeral of her daughter Josephine, even details such as the time and place, may be entirely private. She appreciates the fact that information concerning Mr. Kipling is of public interest, but this sorrow is her own and she feels sure that newspaper reporters and editors will not wish to intrude on her privacy. There are a number of reasons Mrs. Kipling was induced to make this decision, but it is her strong desire that the death of Josephine pass as quickly and quietly as possible for Mr. Kipling's sake . . . '

[*Sound of typing continues then fades*

[*Blackout*

Scene Twenty

[*Extract from* **Martha Pitcher**'*s diary*]

Martha Pitcher [*centre stage in spotlight*] After Josephine's cremation, we all had to play a game, a game of pretend. Family, friends, hotel staff, reporters – we all knew, but we didn't tell. When Mrs Kipling returned from the funeral that afternoon she went straight to see her husband. She disguised the black of her mourning clothes with a colourful shawl. She knew – only too well – but she didn't tell. I assumed I'd be let go in due course, but no, this wasn't to be. Not yet. My staying by the patient's bedside, my typing, was an important part of the game. Anything else, would arouse suspicion. About a week later, it came quite without warning. My last moments in the Kiplings' world. I don't know why but I had the thought that morning that Kipling might like to see my work, the typed record I'd been keeping of his dreams. It just didn't seem right to hand them to him directly so I decided Doubleday would be the best conduit. As I approached his room I heard a woman in distress – sobbing – and the sound of Doubleday's voice offering calm but sharp reassurance.

[*Blackout*

Scene Twenty-One

[*The corridor outside* **Frank Doubleday**'*s hotel room*]

Enter **Caroline Kipling** *and* **Frank Doubleday**

Caroline Kipling I can't Frank! I can't do it anymore . . . !

Frank Doubleday But you're strong Carrie! Sure you can!

Caroline Kipling Everyday this huge weight gets heavier and heavier . . . the LIE . . . don't you see, it's crushing me! Like a dam that's going . . . that's going to burst. [*Pause*] When she first . . . when she left us . . . and he was so ill . . .

Frank Doubleday Carrie . . .

Caroline Kipling It was the *right* thing to do.

Frank Doubleday Let's just take our time . . .

Caroline Kipling Now, *it's not,* Frank. Now, *it's not.*

Frank Doubleday He's not out of the woods yet. I showed you Dr. Janeway's assessment yesterday . . .

Caroline Kipling You have to do it, Frank . . .

Frank Doubleday *I* . . .

Caroline Kipling You do it or I will! But I'll do it badly, you know I will.

Frank Doubleday Can only be from his wife . . . the mother of his child . . .

Caroline Kipling He'll hate me forever! [*Beat*] I know it. I know him. How he deals with his . . . feelings!

Frank Doubleday He won't . . . [*Sighs*]

Caroline Kipling [*weeping*] Better from you Frank, from another man. His Effendi . . .

Martha Pitcher [*aside*] Until this moment I'd been frozen to the spot, listening, but it was that word Effendi . . . that personal name. Suddenly I was aware I was eavesdropping on an intensely private conversation. This was not intended for my ears and my being outside the door was acutely dangerous. I scuttled back to my room. No more than fifteen minutes later there was a sharp knock on my door. On the other side of the door was a freshly composed Doubleday.

Frank Doubleday Gather your things, Martha. Mr. McClure needs you uptown.

Martha Pitcher Am I leaving?

Frank Doubleday Yes.

Martha Pitcher For good?

Frank Doubleday Yes. [*Beat*] Mrs. Kipling has given me the task of breaking the news to her husband. Dr. Janeway does not advise it. We tried . . . Dr. Conland last night and I, this morning . . . to dissuade her but . . .

Martha Pitcher I see. [*Beat*] One cannot blame her. [*Beat*] I don't know how she's managed 'til now.

Frank Doubleday Well, it's not for us to . . . er . . . I must make haste. No sense in waiting . . .

Martha Pitcher Oh, I nearly forgot. [*Giving* **Doubleday** *her pages*] Would you give these pages to Mr. Kipling please?

Frank Doubleday Your typing.

Martha Pitcher Everything's there. Every word.

Frank Doubleday Indeed. [*Leafing through the pages and reading to himself*] 'That small theatre of the brain which we keep brightly lighted all night long.'

Martha Pitcher Robert Louis Stevenson.

Frank Doubleday Indeed! [*Beat*] I'll make sure Mr. Kipling gets the pages, Martha. They may just prove a welcome distraction in the coming days.

[*Exit* **Frank Doubleday**

Scene Twenty-Two

[*The final extract from* **Martha Pitcher***'s diary*]

Martha Pitcher [*centre stage in spotlight*] And with that Doubleday was gone along the corridor and I was spewed on to the Manhattan streets. It was a March morning, crisp and bright. It was odd to be free of the Grenoble and its distinguished occupants, like finally coming up to the surface to breathe. Doubleday had gone that morning to break the news of Josephine's death to Kipling. The story goes he took a seat beside the writer and told the tale in as few words as he could. Kipling listened in silence till Doubleday had finished then turned his face to the wall. In Josephine's memory Kipling made it his mission to record the *Just So Stories,* the tales he created for this daughter. After this, his appetite for writing stories for children ebbed away. He was a sadder and harder man.

[*Music: Debussy's* Clair de Lune, *Debussy* (*1913 recording*)]

Long after the Kiplings left New York I'd walk through Central Park to jobs around Manhattan. I'd always feel the eyes of the Grenoble watching me through the trees. I'd never even stoon before Kipling, to catch his eyes, yet I felt so close to understanding his pain. On each occasion, in that park, I would stop dead amongst the trees. I'd be back there, along at Kipling's bedside. Mopping the sweat from his fevered brow and holding his hand through the nightmares. And it hung on me until one morning it became too much. I raised my eyes defiantly to stare down that old grey building. And I was once again in Kipling's room. He was awake and facing me. Looking right at me. 'Martha?' He knew my name. 'Thank you.' He was holding the typed pages, his brown eyes swelling with tears. 'I'd lost her,' he said 'but you bring her back to me. You bring her back to me.'

[*Spotlight fades*

[*Music: final note of Debussy's* Clair de Lune, *Debussy* (*1913 recording*)]

A NECESSARY WOMAN

Written and devised by
Deborah Clair & Philippa Urquhart

Dedicated to Emily Wilding Davison
and all the unsung heroines
in Parliament and everywhere . . .

A Necessary Woman

A Necessary Woman was first presented by CLAIR/OBSCUR in the Caryl Churchill Theatre at Royal Holloway, University of London on 7th March 2018.

The play was presented in the Macmillan Room, Portcullis House at the Houses of Parliament on 26th March 2018 to commemorate the centenary of the Representation of the People Act and as a tribute to Emily Wilding Davison, who made the ultimate sacrifice for the Cause at the Epsom Derby two years later.

A Necessary Woman was also performed in the Davison family home of Morpeth on 11th September 2018 on the eve of the unveiling of a new statue of Emily Davison in Carlisle Park.

On all three occasions the play was performed with the following cast and production team:

Emily Davison	Deborah Clair
Mary Tatton	Philippa Urquhart
Directed by	Dominique Gerrard
Sound Design by	Rich Keeble
Costumes by	Georgie Lancaster
Wigs by	Lorraine Collett
Set by	Mick Webb

The March of the Women was written by Cicely Hamilton (1872–1952) and composed by Dame Ethel Smyth (1858–1944). In our production the singer was Jane Kirby.

CLAIR/OBSCUR is a female-led theatre company founded by Deborah Clair to share the stories of remarkable women. The company prides itself on providing opportunities to female creatives, enabling them to tell their own stories faithfully. CLAIR/OBSCUR derives its name from the term *chiaroscuro*, a strong, self-conscious juxtaposition of light and shade.

Authors' Note

A Necessary Woman is a re-imagining of suffragette Emily Davison's protest by hiding in a cleaning cupboard in St Mary's Undercroft in Parliament on Census Night 1911. Emily's residence was recorded as the House of Commons by P. E. Ridge, the Clerk of Works, Houses of Parliament when she was discovered on Monday 3rd April. The play is based on factual evidence gathered from Parliamentary Archives.

As actors working on our script, we found the best staging solution to adequately depict the cleaning cupboard, which did not interfere with audience sightlines, was to mark the cupboard area with three wooden crates and to construct a solid door frame with an imaginary door. The opening and closing of the door is always mimed so all action and reactions are clearly seen by the audience.

During our research for this play two significant discoveries were made. The first was that Emily intended to hide in the House of Commons and to make a speech during Prime Minister's Questions. Emily's final speech in ***A Necessary Woman*** was developed from the actual speech she intended to make in Parliament on Monday 3rd April 1911.

The second was a discovery made by Deborah Clair of previously unidentified film footage of Emily Davison on a march in June 1910 in the BFI film archives. Until this discovery the only known film footage of the suffragette was of her fatal actions at the Epsom Derby on 4th June 1913.

Deborah Clair and Philippa Urquhart

A Note about Emily's speech

In her original speech Emily referred to 'women of England.' There is, however, freedom to change 'England' to 'Great Britain' or 'Britain' as was done when the play was performed at the Edinburgh Festival Fringe in 2018 (see pages 24, 40 and 41 below).

Characters

Emily Davison a member of the Women's Social and Political Union

Mary Tatton a maid in Speaker Lowther's household

Scene One

St Mary's Chapel Undercroft, Palace of Westminster, Friday 31st March 1911, a quarter to five in the afternoon.

[*House lights down to black*

Sounds of protest, shouting, a window being smashed. The final guided tour of the day can be heard being ushered up the undercroft stairs. The lights go out and there is the sound of a key turning in a lock.

Enter **Emily**

[*She emerges into the half-light from the shadows, creeps across to the cupboard, mimes opening the door, takes her hat off and enters the cupboard. There are three crates, a tin bucket and a polish box in the cupboard.* **Emily** *barricades the door with boxes. She unbuttons her coat, removes her feather boa and tucks this and her gloves away. Opening her bag she removes a lamp and places it on the floor. Taking out matches, she lights the lamp and then raises it into view and places it on a crate.* **Emily** *settles herself and begins to pray.*]

Emily Saint Joan of Arc, patron of France, my patron saint, I ask you now to fight this battle with me by prayer, just as you led your troops to victory in battle. You, who were filled with the Holy Spirit and chosen by God, help me this day with the favour I ask. Grant me by your divine and powerful intercession, the courage and strength I need to endure this constant fight. Oh St. Joan, help me to be victorious in the tasks God presents to me.

[*Big Ben strikes five o'clock in the afternoon. Sounds of* **Emily**, *who has fallen asleep. She begins to murmur and fret and this gradually grows in intensity to full-blown nightmare. A jangling of keys offstage. A dim light illuminates the chapel undercroft from the outer area of St Stephen's Hall. Sound of footsteps slowly descending stairs*]

Enter **Mary**

[*The dark figure of a woman, moving slowly and deliberately across the stage. The figure, now distinguishable as* **Mary** *flops into a wooden upright chair for a breather. It is now the morning of Saturday 1st April*]

Mary Can't see a bleedin' thing in 'ere!

[*Exit* **Mary**, *going off to turn the light on at the bottom of the stairs*

[*Lighting change*

Enter **Mary**

[*Wearily, she sits back down on the chair, rubs her aching foot and groans.* **Mary** *hears a similar murmur from behind which startles her but dismisses this as her imagination. She decides to move to the cupboard to find what she came for*]

Mary Come on Mary, no such thing as ghosts! [*Not quite believing it*] Not even the ghost of Guy Fawkes. Brasso! [*She approaches the cupboard*]

Emily [*shouting*] Nooooooo!

Mary Oooohh!

Emily [*shouting*] Leave me alone!

Mary [*taking fright, calling*] Mr Bennett!!

Emily [*shouting*] I shall be sick!!

Mary [*returning cautiously*] What's that? Who's in there?

[*Silence*]

Mary [*cautiously*] Is anyone in there??

[*Sound of someone kicking a metal pail. Taking courage,* **Mary** *picks up a mop and braces herself*]

Mary Come out and show yourself!

[*Silence*]

Mary Right. [**Mary** *steels herself and marches towards the cupboard door, tries the handle, the door doesn't budge*] What?! What on earth? Open this door! [**Mary** *pushes as hard as she can and the door opens an inch, but is very abruptly pushed back*] Flamin' 'eck! [*Pause*] Who's in there? [*Silence*] Who are you? Open this door! [*She pushes the door again*] Right then, I'm off to report this . . .

Emily [*with great intensity*] Beloved Saint Joan. Protect me.

Mary Who? Joan – who?

Emily I am Saint Joan!

Mary What's going on?

Emily I'm fighting for justice.

Mary Flamin' 'eck!

Emily Justice! For me, for you, for all women!

Mary How on earth did you get in 'ere?

Emily It wasn't difficult.

Mary Are you one of them, a suffragette?

Emily I am Saint Joan!

Mary Saint Joan? Not Queen Victoria then?

Emily Of course not!

Mary Oh . . . you've come from Bedlam have you? The 'ospital, have you?

Emily No, I haven't!

Mary You're Joan, are you?

Emily Joan is a woman in a man's world. She is my eternal inspiration.

Mary Oh, I see. Well dear, you won't find no inspiration in there, will you? I'll just go and fetch Mr Bennett, he'll be able to help you . . .

Emily *Please, please.* I must remain undiscovered until Monday morning.

Mary Monday! Why??

Emily You must know what's happening on Sunday night.

Mary Sunday? [*Penny drops*] Oh! You're one of *them*, are you? Suffragette. Well I dunno what your game is, but I know what's happening *Saturday* night – tonight – and I need to get in this cupboard! Brasso, silver polish. [*Walking off*] I'm off to get Mr Bennett!

Emily Wait – please don't go! What's your name?

Mary I'm sorry, Miss. [*Leaving*]

Emily I'll do . . . anything.

Mary [**Emily's** *tone causes* **Mary** *to stop dead*] What? To stay in this cupboard? What for?

Emily [*pause*] What's your name?

Mary My *name??* [*Softening*] My name's Mary Tatton.

Emily Mary.

Mary Mary, Miss.

Emily Mary?

Mary Yes, Miss?

Emily Do you really *have* to get into this cupboard?

Mary Yes, I do Miss! It's my master's birthday today and we've got his party to prepare for.

Emily But Sunday night . . .

Mary We're out of brass and silver polish and I've been told there's some in here. All the doorplates need doing and all the silverware! I gotta get in there! Open this door! [*Pushes door*]

Emily Do you know what Sunday night is?

Mary 'course I do. It's Census Night, but my master takes care of all that. Nothing to do with me, I don't count. Look Miss, I gotta get this stuff, I gotta lot to do!

Emily Your master?

Mary Mr Lowther.

Emily Mr Lowther?

Mary Mr Lowther, Speaker of the House of Commons. In case you didn't know.

Emily As it happens, I do know. I'm also aware of Mr Lowther's views on women's suffrage.

Mary Well, Miss . . .

Emily Sunday is Census Night. Thousands of us women are uniting in our refusal to submit to this. We'll be hiding in darkened houses, barricading the doors, defacing our Census forms . . .

Mary But why, Miss? It's just a few names on a page. Mr Lowther thinks it's a good thing, he says it'll be an 'elp. What harm can it do?

Emily *Harm?* Women must be included in the shaping of our future. Yes, this Census is intended to provide information so that the Government can improve the living conditions of ordinary working people. But, Mary who knows *more* about the difficulties of domestic affairs than women – disease, hunger, destitution – and who knows *less* about their hardships than those gentlemen sitting in Parliament? *That's* the harm, that's the hypocrisy! Why should the millions of women in this land comply with the Government's request for information when they allow us no voice or means to express our views? We are invisible, we do not count, therefore we shall not be counted.

[*Sound of footsteps above. The women freeze*]

Emily What's that?

Mary Ssh!

[*They hear the undercroft door creaking open*]

Emily [*whispering*] *Please . . .*

Mary [*shouting up the stairs*] Morning, Mr Bennett, it's all right, it's just me, Mary, from Speaker's House. Just fetchin' some Brasso and silver polish. [*Pause*]

Mr Bennett [*offstage*] Very well, just don't forget the key.

Mary Right you are Mr Bennett, I'll return the key to the Sergeant's office.

[*Sound of door closing and* **Mr Bennett** *walking away*]

Emily [*pause*] Thank you.

Mary S'cuse me Miss, but couldn't you find a more convenient place to hide?

Emily Oh, this is only the first part of my mission, *I have a greater purpose* ——

Mary What's that then?

Emily On Monday morning a woman's voice will be heard, it will be heard in the Ho ——

Mary Right miss. I need my stuff. I've got me work to do and they'll be wondering where I am. If I'm here much longer, I'll be in trouble. Look, in that cupboard, on your right, not on the shelf, but on the floor beneath it – there's a box of polishes . . . now . . .

Emily Can I trust you?

Mary Trust! I've had enough of this [*marching to the door, shouting*] Give me my polish! [*Realising she's being too loud, quieter*] Give me my polish!

[*In the meantime,* **Emily** *has moved the boxes and has the box of polishes in her hand.* **Mary** *walks away from the door in order to take a running shove. As* **Mary** *turns, the door suddenly opens six inches and* **Emily** *thrusts out the box of polish*]

Mary Oh [*slightly put out*] much obliged. [**Mary** *makes to leave, but lingers*] Look Miss, what you're doing is your business and I want no part of it. But, if you want to change your mind, you could leave with me, now? The tours will be starting soon, but I reckon I can get you out now, while it's quiet.

Emily No thank you, Mary. [*Beat*] It's necessary that I stay.

Mary You said Monday?

Emily 'til Monday.

Mary [*walks off into the cloakroom and returns with a cup of water*] Look Miss, Monday morning's a long way off. There's a cloakroom through there. Here's some water, if you're thirsty. [*Places mug on the chair*]

Emily [*pause*] Mary, will you keep this a secret? [*Beat*] Do I have your word?

Mary No, I can't give you my word – bloody hell! S'cuse me, Miss. [*Pause*] Well Miss, I haven't seen yer, have I? I dunno you're 'ere. Could be the ghost of Guy Fawkes . . . [*Walks up the steps*]

[*Exit* **Mary**, *locking the door*

[**Emily** *listens and waits a beat to make sure* **Mary** *has gone. Then she opens the door, races out of the cupboard, grabs the mug and quickly consumes the water*]

[*Blackout*

Scene Two

Sunday morning – 2nd April

Music: part of the final verse of The March of the Women [*distant and ethereal*] *begins*

Light from the stained-glass window gradually fades up on **Emily**, *kneeling on a prayer stool downstage. She sees in her prayer her vision of St. Joan. She seems to be having a restorative experience of some kind.*

Enter **Mary**, *halfway through the song*

[*Holding the polish box* **Mary** *stands watching* **Emily**]

Emily (*singing*) *Life, strife – these two are one,*
Naught can ye win but by faith and daring;
On, on, that ye have done
But for the work of today preparing.

[*Towards the end of the song,* **Mary** *retreats*]

[*Exit* **Mary**

[**Emily** *stands up and stretches*]

Emily Thoughts have gone forth whose powers can sleep no more!

[**Mary** *can be heard making her presence felt offstage*]

Enter **Mary**

[**Mary** *is carrying the box of polishes. She stands a moment*]

Mary Are you here, Miss?

[*Silence.* **Mary** *cautiously goes to the cupboard and taps on the door*]

Mary Miss? It's Mary.

Emily From Speaker's House?

Mary Yes.

Emily What day is it?

Mary It's Sunday morning – early, Miss.

Emily Census Night, tonight.

Mary Yes, Miss.

Emily One more day, one more night . . .

Mary Then you can go home.

Emily I doubt if I shall be going home.

Mary Why's that, Miss?

Emily Because on Monday morning I will be in the House of Commons.

Mary You can't do that, Miss.

Emily I can.

Mary No, you can't

Emily Yes, I can.

Mary They closed the Ladies' Gallery after that Australian actress chained herself to the grille, and they took hours to free her from it. Special entry only now. She's spoilt it for the lot of you. Went to Holloway Prison for a month she did.

Emily I intend to enter the House itself.

Mary You can't.

Emily I can. I can and I will.

Mary Don't even try those tricks in the House of Commons, Miss. Is there nothin' sacred to you? It's Parliament! I know what you lot have done to St Stephen's Hall, up there [*gesturing, angrily*]. Painting all over the walls, breaking bits off the statues. That's not right. And you know what they do to your women in the streets – man-handled, thrown to the ground, beaten – by the crowds, by the police. You don't want to be treated like that, Miss . . .

Emily I've known worse.

Mary What worse, Miss?

Emily In prison.

Mary [*shocked*] You've been to prison, Miss?

Emily Yes; I consider it an honour.

Mary An honour – it's a disgrace!

Emily I consider it the greatest honour to fight for women's freedom. What nobler cause could there be?

Mary What did they put you in for?

Emily Obstruction, stone throwing, smashing windows.

Mary Well, I think you suffragettes should stop throwing your weight about. Throwing stones, smashing people's windows, shouting in the street! You're a bloody nuisance. S'cuse me Miss. Have you any idea how many men it took to free that woman from the grille? Six! Tell me this, when you're doing your smashing, do you ever think about the poor sod who's gotta clear it up? And who's paying for it – not you lot! You should be ashamed!

Emily I am *not* ashamed. I have already paid for it by sacrificing friends, family, my health – you have no idea the brutality we receive in prison – my good name. *My good name.* In this humiliation, I suffer most.

Mary What happened in prison then?

Emily I can't . . . speak about that.

[*Pause.* **Emily** *clearly upset and* **Mary** *doesn't know what to say, but listens*]

Emily [*after a long pause*] You think I'm mad, don't you? You think, why would any woman in their right mind behave in this way and how dare someone of my privilege go on about suffering when many would argue I have never really known it? And you would be right, in part; I have money or the means to make it and I have always had a roof over my head, enough food to eat and never gone barefoot. But what you also need to understand is that I'm fighting for all women to have a voice, for me and for you, Mary. The moment is now, Mary. This Census is supposed to help bring about change for those in need, but . . .

Mary That's just what Mr Lowther said . . .

Emily Women *need* the vote. You can tell them what's needed, Mary to make things better. You know more than they do, you do count. Your vote could be very important, more than that – vital, necessary. For you, for me, for our children, for our children's children . . .

Mary My dad worked down the docks. My family were poor, very poor. I had eight brothers and sisters, but three of them died. Diphtheria, typhoid. In the winter, we was sent out to beg for coal. Living was hard. I didn't want to leave home, but it was one less mouth for my mum and dad to feed. Coming into service has been a better life for me.

Emily My life – was different – I was comfortable. I worked as a governess. A good family, beautiful surroundings, but I longed to get back to London, the centre of the universe.

Mary Yes Miss, I know what you mean, the centre of the universe.

Emily In the beginning I was intrigued by – although somewhat disapproving of – the suffragette movement. I was curious about the WSPU meetings. The photographs in the newspapers showed such a brightness in the eyes of the campaigners. They were alive! They weren't living a humdrum existence, trapped by their employment or position. And the articles that followed these pictures, the unfavourable claims and assertions made about these women – couldn't possibly be right. I had to see for myself. I chose my first meeting with none other than Mrs Pankhurst herself to speak.

Mary [*impressed*] Mrs Pankhurst . . .

Emily There was a hush in the hall as she swept on to the stage. The group of young girls in front were almost swooning. This was not for a matinee idol, not for a man. [*Laughs*] Mrs Pankhurst is charming, handsome – yes, but she's a *woman*. A married, middle-aged woman!

Mary [*laughing*] Well I never!

Emily And then she spoke: 'We are here, not because we are law-breakers; we are here in our efforts to become law-makers.' Silence. You could hear a pin drop. Then the room shook with applause.

Mary So what did you do then?

Emily I joined them. There and then.

Mary And these other refined ladies, do they think it's right to break the law?

Emily We don't want to break the law. For years we have campaigned peacefully and we've got nowhere, we've been ignored. We are fighting for a better future for all. We break the law as a last resort, it is the only way, it's necessary. There will come a time when women will no longer be constrained, no longer cabined and confined!

Mary Well you can always open the door, Miss. What does Mrs Pankhurst think about you doing this, shutting yourself in cupboards?

Emily Actually, she doesn't know I'm here. I act alone.

Mary Well, you're a very naughty girl – how can bring yourself to behave like this?

Emily When I break the law it's not *me*. One has to step outside oneself, do you see? When I go home my mother always says: 'Emily, what have you been doing? I have seen such and such a thing in the paper and I know you were in it.' I reply: 'But how can you? When I am going to do anything, I always put you quite away from me, quite out of my mind.' I call it being under the influence. Steel yourself and then you can do anything.

Mary Your mother's your mother! You might put thoughts of her out your mind, but that don't stop her wondering and worrying about you. You're deliberately putting yourself in harm's way.

Emily Yes I am and there is a heavy price to pay for breaking the law – when you walk through the gates of a prison; you die!

Mary You *die?*

Emily You cease to be a person. No one talks to you, except to issue an order and you must not speak to another soul.

Mary Not speak?

Emily You'd be amazed what you try and read into a snatched glance from an inmate; what comfort there is from a few words scratched on a cell wall. When you come out, back into the real world, nothing appears to have changed – the people go about just the same, the buses buzz along the streets, but you know things have changed forever. You hear questions, you hear yourself respond, but you're hovering outside yourself; you're dead.

Mary You really want to do these things?

Emily This is my mission. I dedicate my life to it. I have no choice in this matter.

Mary Miss Emily . . . you were praying earlier . . .

Emily To St. Joan. [*Beat*] She talks to me.

Mary What does she say?

Emily She gives me strength, she gives me hope, she sustains me.

Mary I think you need something to eat, Miss.

Emily I'll not be fed again . . . [*crash from the cupboard as* **Emily** *faints and falls off the boxes*]

Mary Miss??

[**Mary** *rushes to the cupboard and tries to push the door open, but* **Emily***'s weight against the door prevents this*]

Mary Are you all right? [*Shouting*] Emily!

Emily [*murmuring incoherently*] Not by the *junior* doctor . . .

Mary You're up against the door – I can't move it! [*Noises of agony from the cupboard*] Oh Lord!! Help – Mr Ben—!! [*Rushes to get more water*] More water here, Miss! Don't worry, I'll be back soon!

[**Mary** *rushes up the stairs as Big Ben chimes eight o'clock in the morning*]

[*Exit* **Mary**

[*Lights fade*

Scene Three

Sunday morning – 2nd April – about eleven o'clock

Enter **Emily**

[*She wanders on from the side with some water, a pencil and notebook. She is composing the speech she intends to make in the House of Commons on Monday morning*]

Emily Gentlemen of the House of Commons, I address you on behalf of all the women of England . . . no [*crossing out vigorously*] I ask you – no, too weak! I implore you? Women of England demand [*discovers the light of St. Joan and this provides the sudden inspiration*] Do *justice* to the women of England by passing the Women's Enfranchisement Bill in 1911! [**Emily** *raises her cup to St. Joan*] Thank you! [*Takes a sip of water and then lowers the cup and prays*] St. Joan – my refuge and strength, a very present help in trouble. Therefore, I will not fear though the earth be removed and the mountains be carried into the midst of the sea!

[**Emily** *hears the jangling of keys, re-enters the cupboard, closes the door, perches on boxes with her foot up against the door frame*]

Enter **Mary** *approaching the cupboard cautiously*

Mary [*quietly*] Miss? Miss Emily? Are you there, Miss Emily?

Emily Mary ——?

Mary Thank the Lord, Miss – are you all right? I think you fainted. I left some water by the door, here – did you find it?

Emily Yes, thank you, Mary. It was a great help.

Mary It's me day off today. I just came over earlier to return these bits, but you weren't well so I come back – brought you something to eat.

Emily What is it, Mary?

Mary Something sweet – give me your hand, give me your hand! [**Emily** *slowly opens a crack in the door and puts her hand out*] A treat. [**Mary** *puts a piece of wrapped cake in* **Emily***'s hand*]

Emily Oh – cake!

Mary Mr Lowther's birthday cake – we've all had a piece.

Emily Oh Mary – thank you! [*Eats a mouthful*] It's delicious, will you share it with me?

Mary It's for you, Miss.

Emily [*handing some back*] Let's share it.

Mary Oh – much obliged, I'm sure, Miss! [*Sitting down on the prayer stool*]

[*They eat.* **Emily** *coughs*]

Mary You can taste the brandy, can't you?

Emily [*laughing*] Eating his cake now . . . Mr Lowther doesn't like me very much!

Mary How do you mean, Miss?

Emily Have you heard of the Index Expurgatorius?

Mary Index Expurger – bloody hell! Sorry Miss. No, I ain't – what is it?

Emily It's a list of undesirable nuisances who are not welcome here. Mr Lowther decides who they are.

Mary I see . . .

[*Silence as they eat*]

Mary They give you cake in prison?

Emily [*she suddenly stops eating, wraps up the cake*] No, nothing like that.

Mary Well, what did they give you then?

Emily It's WSPU policy to refuse food as soon as you go in.

Mary So they gave it to you, but you wouldn't eat it?

[*Silence*]

Emily If you don't eat it, they force it on you.

Mary They force it on you?

Emily They won't recognise us as political prisoners . . .

Mary You've gotta eat, you'll starve.

Emily It's the most powerful tool, the only one we have in there . . .

Mary Why don't you just close your mouth?

Emily Mary – there's so much you don't know. They find a way. [*Pause*] Half a dozen wardresses come into your cell with the doctors. 'I am going to feed you by force.' They hold you down so you can't move. They lie you flat or tie you to a chair. If you don't open your mouth, the doctor (a junior one if you're unlucky), forces it with a steel gag and screws it wide open. The doctor tried all round my mouth with a steel gag to find an opening. On the right side of my mouth there two teeth are missing, here. He found this gap, pushed in the gag, prised open my mouth to its widest extent, then forced two feet of rubber tube down my throat. At the top of the tube is a funnel. A wardress poured liquid down my throat out of a tin enameled cup.

[***Mary*** *looks at the tin enameled water cup that has been left on the chair*]

Mary That must be terrible . . . what's in the cup?

Emily Raw eggs, milk and some foul medicament. [*Slight pause,* **Mary** *wraps the last of her cake up, no longer hungry for it*] It was a horror. The memory of it will haunt me for the rest of my life.

[*Sound of footsteps approaching quickly from above*]

Mary I left the keys outside in the lock!! [**Mary** *dashes to retrieve them, but only gets to the bottom of the stairs*]

Constable 'ello? Keys in the lock?

[**Mary** *rushes back.* **Emily** *opens the cupboard door and reaches her hand out to* **Mary** *who scrambles inside.* **Mary** *squeezes past to hide behind* **Emily** *who shuts the cupboard door. The undercroft door creaks open*]

Constable [*offstage*] 'ello – anybody there? No. Someone's for it. [*Shouting*] It's all right Mr Bennett, no one here. [*Sound of keys turning in the lock*] Reckon it's time for my cuppa . . .

[*They listen as the* **Constable** *walks away*]

Mary [*in the darkness of the cupboard*] Locked it! He's locked it! I'm shut in! Oh Lord – what have I done. I'll be in so much trouble.

Emily Mary, Mary – you've done nothing.

Mary I can't stay here, Miss. I work for Mr Lowther. [*Pushes past* **Emily** *and out of the cupboard back into the undercroft*] It's Census Night, I gotta be back by six! [*Shouting*] Help!

[**Emily** *rushes out of the cupboard and attempts to calm* **Mary** *down*]

Emily Mary, Mary . . . it'll be all right! We'll find a way – let's think . . .

Mary I'm done for . . .

Emily No, let's think . . . you got locked in by mistake; you were in the cloakroom and didn't hear the man call . . .

Mary Supposed to be at my sister's . . .

Emily You called after him, ran up the stairs, but he'd gone . . .

Mary I was taken ill and I missed the omnibus . . .

Emily You fainted down here and bumped your head . . .

Mary Her little girl was taken ill and I had to stay with her while me sister went off to fetch the doctor . . .

Emily I locked you in and held you hostage . . .

Mary I could . . . [**Mary** *looks at* **Emily** *properly for the first time, the penny drops*] . . . red hair . . .

Emily Yes . . .

Mary You're the redhead.

Emily What do you mean?

Mary I've seen you before.

Emily Possibly, I'm here quite a lot.

Mary I know who you are . . . you're on that list . . . Oh my Lord! You're an . . . undesirable!

[*Lights fade as Big Ben ticks on . . .*

Scene Four

A few hours have passed. It is now four o'clock on Sunday afternoon. Lights up on **Emily** *seated on prayer stool with her carpet bag next to her. The notes for* **Emily***'s speech are all over the floor.*

Mary *comes slowly across the undercroft floor from the door*

Emily How many times have you tried that door now, Mary?

Mary Well, if someone should happen to unlock it, it'd be better for the both of us.

[**Mary** *doesn't sit down, but continues to pace the floor, anxiously. Big Ben chimes four o'clock. The women count the chimes to determine the time of day*]

Mary [*to herself*] Could say the omnibus broke down or me sister was taken ill . . . so I got 'numerated there . . . ?

Emily My plan remains unaltered, Mary.

Mary Oh yes, the speech in the Commons. Still on that, Miss?

Emily Still on that. It's nearly finished, but not quite. It needs more punch, I need to make it personal.

Mary Even, if by some miracle you manage to get in there, Miss, four policemen will seize you and cart you out before you can open your mouth.

Emily Not if I'm attached to the chamber itself! [**Emily** *raises a lock and chain from her open carpet bag*]

Mary Oh Lord!

[**Emily** *laughs*]

Mary [*angrily*] This is just a big joke to you, is it? Do you think for a minute about the lives you're wreckin'? There'll be questions asked of us when they find you, jobs on the line. Families wrecked! Is that personal enough for you, Miss?

Emily Mary ——

Mary I will lose my job, after forty-three years of service. I will lose my job because I helped yer, because I felt sorry for yer, because I was worried [*breaking*] that you'd die, on your own in this undercroft.

Emily Mary, you must know how grateful ——

Mary I don't want your thanks – what use is that to me? All right, Mr Lowther doesn't want the likes of you 'ere and you don't like Mr Lowther or what Mr Lowther thinks. So, it's fun for you to play tricks and hide in cupboards to make your point. To me, Mr Lowther is . . . family. I've worked for the family since I was a girl of fourteen, when this Speaker Lowther was still at Eton. I'm fifty-eight years old now, so it's been a long time. I've never worked for anyone else, and I'm sure I wouldn't know how to now... [**Mary** *sinks down into the chair*]

Emily That is a long time.

Mary It's a life time. [*After a pause*] What I do is light the fires in the morning and do any cleaning I'm asked. It's a very busy day, 'specially in the winter. I'm a Necessary Woman, Miss, and I am necessary that's for sure. I'm the one that does the fires. No one knows how to light a fire better than I do. Master always says: 'I need to be warm Mary, I cannot work, I cannot think straight, unless I'm warm!' I got my own special way to twist and loop the paper, so it's right. It's my special way, old newspaper, that's what I use. Can't use too much though, otherwise you'd smother the flame, you got to build in the kindling. Just small little sticks of wood, so you've got a pile, like a little mountain, built so the air can get through. Because that's what a fire needs – air. Then, you can put a match to it and when that little mountain of kindle gets going and it's flaming away, then you build your coal into it – see my hands, Miss? That's because of the coal, it don't go away now, even when I scrub them, that's coal dust that is – but now you got to watch it, you got to watch it! You turn around at all or just take your eyes off it, and it'll go out. It'll escape you, it's gone! And then you'll have to start again. Keep your eyes on it, and then when the coal catches proper you can add more, and then perhaps more. That's called banking it up. So, then it lasts and the room's getting warmer and warmer. It's magic really, how it all changes, and that's because of me, I know how.

Emily You're a valuable woman, Mary.

Mary Well I suppose I am, Miss Emily, in that! [*Pause*] I'm a necessary woman. I get up at half past four every morning to light those flaming fires... all day long I'm tending them, keeping them *alive*!

Emily You've been very loyal to the Lowthers.

Mary Well I have Miss. And they've been very good to me. [*Pause*] You see, Miss, years ago – I worked for old Mr Lowther, then. I hadn't been working for them that long really – I got into a bit of trouble, I was young and foolish Miss, and so ashamed, and I was desperate. At first, it weren't noticeable so I could keep it quiet, but I knew that wouldn't last. I'd have to say something. In the end I told the Housekeeper how it was and she took me straight to the Mistress. It were terrible, I could hardly bring myself to speak about it.

Emily What happened then?

Mary Well, the Mistress was very kind. She found somewhere for me to be while I had the baby. But she had to speak to Mr Lowther of course. I thought I'd never see them again, but after it was all over they had me back. They had me back! So I started working for them again, and I was so grateful. It was as though nothing had ever happened.

Emily And your . . . *baby*?

Mary I wasn't supposed to know, but one of the nurses told me it was a girl. A little girl. I was told she'd be up for adoption. Up for adoption. So, she's around somewhere. And living a better life than I could have given her I'm sure. I called her Daisy but no one knew that. My Daisy. But of course, that's not her name now.

Emily She would be about my age?

Mary She would.

Emily She could be a suffragette!

Mary Well, Miss Emily, I never thought of that. [*Pause*] She wouldn't dare!

[**Emily** *starts to pick up her scattered speech papers from the floor*]

Mary Look Miss, I know what you're doing is important to you, but they've been good to me, the Lowthers and now I've let them down again.

Emily You were only doing what you thought was right.

Mary But when they find out, find us here – together, they won't see things that way. I should've reported it, from the word go, sorry Miss.

Emily I'm so glad you didn't.

Mary You want to get caught tomorrow though, don't you? I just want to keep my job. I still might if I could just get out of here – no one will have missed me yet, 'cept me sister, I was supposed to see her today.

Emily When will they be raising the alarm – after six?

Mary The 'numerator's coming to call. Mr Lowther made such a big thing about it, gave all the staff a lecture on the importance of the Census, before his party last night. A five pound fine, they're saying if you miss it. Five pounds! Wherever will I find that? Mr Lowther was very serious . . .

Emily Was he?

Mary He was, but he was in a joking – how do you say it?

Emily Jocular?

Mary Jocular mood.

Emily I suppose it was his birthday . . .

[*They look at each other and smile*]

Emily You said you know me?

Mary I've seen you before. I recognise the red hair, now you're out of your hiding place. I saw you last year. You were being led out by a couple of policemen, across Old Palace Yard. You looked . . . you were covered in dust and dirt!

Emily I'd been hiding somewhere else that day – in a ventilation shaft.

Mary A ventilation shaft? Where –? How on earth did you get in there?

Emily Luck really. I was on the end of a tour moving through the Great Central Hall. There was a little passage beyond it, tried a door which was unlocked. There was a policeman, but at that moment he was looking the wrong way, so I slipped in. In the wall of the corridor beyond, there was a little glass window that led to the ventilation shaft. I crawled in.

Mary And no one found you?

Emily No – there was a series of ladders going higher into the tower. I reached the first platform with difficultly and perched there. It was very uncomfortable and dangerous. I was terrified of falling off.

Mary Flamin' 'eck!

Emily I hid there for almost twenty-eight hours. Was very dirty and dusty and the pipes made it terribly hot.

Mary You looked like a little chimney sweep, when I saw you. Thought a bit of luck might be coming my way . . .

Emily I was slightly better prepared in that I had some food – chocolate and bananas – but I couldn't last because I desperately needed water.

Mary 'course you needed water!

Emily I came out of the shaft and found a little tap right there in the wall.

Mary Oh my Lord, thank goodness!

Emily The sign next to the tap said 'Cold'.

Mary Oh Miss . . .

Emily Water's never tasted so good! After that I could have waited in that shaft for days . . . dozing off, listening out for the chimes of Big Ben and the afternoon bells of the Abbey, footsteps . . .

Mary Miss – you could've died.

Emily Could have been locked in, could have died of thirst, fallen off the platform . . .

[**Mary** *looks at* **Emily**. **Mary** *is silent*]

Emily In the end, it was the *water* that gave me away.

Mary How's that, Miss?

Emily Constable came past on his rounds and must have seen the water on the floor. All of a sudden the door opened and he looked in. I must have looked ghastly covered in grime, a terrible apparition! He was trembling so much he nearly dropped his lantern. He shouted 'What is it?', banged the door back and blew his whistle. Another constable came and they carted me off to be washed . . .

Mary That must have been when I saw yer. You were such a sight – I remember! Is that when they put you on the blacklist?

Emily Soon after that. I broke some windows in the Crown Office . . .

Mary 'Silly woman!' That's what Mr Lowther said. I heard him talking about it to the Serjeant-at-Arms: 'What did she hope to achieve?' 'Nothing, but making herself uncomfortable and look ridiculous . . . '

Emily Well, I certainly looked ridiculous.

Mary Yes Miss.

Emily [*looking at* **Mary**] Not as if they have never seen a woman covered in dust before . . .

Mary No Miss . . . [*Pause*] On your own, in the dark all the time, no one to help yer. You gotta lot of pluck, Miss. I don't know how you keep going.

Emily I keep going because . . . I have to. I've told you before, it's not a matter of choice. I am inspired by the shining light of St. Joan. Hers was a life of action in which she broke all the rules. I *will* follow this path to wherever it takes me. Through my humble work in this noblest of all causes, I have become fulfilled. I am blessed! I have an interest in living which I've never experienced before. What would I do now, anyway, if I wasn't a suffragette? I dare say I could work as a governess again; no.

Mary So, you sacrificed everything for your cause. You must have great faith that you'll win; you've given up your life to fight for it.

Emily I have faith in my mission. Courage, persistence, determination. Persistence – that's the key.

Mary Headstrong, wilful, rebellious, naughty – that's been your key!

[***Emily** laughs heartily*]

Mary [*remembering*] Key . . . spare key . . . spare key . . .

Emily [*jumping up after* **Mary**] Spare key – is there one? Do you know that?

Mary Sometimes there's all night vigils down 'ere. That's why they have the cloakroom. One of the Members got locked in one night by mistake so after that they had to leave a spare key . . .

[*They frantically search for a spare key.* **Mary** *rushes out into the corridor,* **Emily** *rushes into the cupboard. Both find nothing. Moment of realisation – they rush into the cloakroom*]

[*Exit* **Emily** *and* **Mary**

Mary [*offstage*] Well I'll be!

Enter **Emily**, *holding the key aloft, followed by* **Mary**

Mary Try it Miss! Try it in the door . . .

[*Exit* **Emily**, *going upstairs to try the key*

[*The key can be heard turning in the lock*]

Enter **Emily**

Emily Door's open – quick, quick!

[**Mary** *starts to leave, but stops to thank St. Joan*]

Mary [*curtsies to St. Joan*] Thank you!!

Emily Quickly!

Mary Thank you, Miss.

Emily Thank you, Mary. You've made *this* stay in Parliament more than bearable.

[*They embrace*]

Emily Go forth and be enumerated!!

[*Exit* **Mary**

[**Emily** *locks the door behind her*]

Enter **Emily**, *holding the key*

[*She is about to put the key in her pocket, but then decides to put it back in the cloakroom*]

[*Exit* **Emily**

Enter **Emily**

[*She purposefully picks up her bag.* **Emily** *dresses in the blackout*]

Scene Five

Early Monday morning – 3rd April – sounds of bells pealing. **Emily** *is putting her gloves on in the cupboard, gathering her things and making her final preparations. She hears* **Mary***'s knocking and then her urgent low whisper.*

Mary [*offstage*] Miss, Miss! Are you there, Miss? Let me in!

[*Exit* **Emily**, *moving swiftly to collect the key from the cloakroom*

Enter **Emily**, *with the key*

[*Exit* **Emily**, *disappearing up the stairs*

Enter **Mary**, *after a moment, rushing in, followed by* **Emily**

Emily What's happened, why are you here again?

Mary Census Night! It's all over the papers!

Emily What do the papers say? Was the boycott a success?

Mary I don't know, Miss, I've no idea, but they reckon there's going to be trouble on College Green this morning. The Serjeant-at-Arms is bringing in special constables in to guard St Stephen's Hall, be all over the place in half an hour. Come with me now Miss and I can get you out!

Emily Mary ——

Mary I can't stay long, Miss. Please, come with me now!

Emily Is the Commons open yet?

Mary I don't know, Miss – Mr Lowther leaves the house at nine o'clock.

Emily Do you think it'll be open for cleaning?

Mary Cleaning?? Listen to me, Emily. You're a brave young woman, but this is foolish. We women need you to speak up for us and continue the fight with your words. How can you do that if you're shut up in jail. It's not good for you Miss, it's not good for us.

Emily I have the words. I just need to be in the Commons to be heard!

[*Sound of constables gathering outside the building, receiving orders*]

Mary They're comin' into St Stephen's Hall, they'll be searching all round here. Come on Miss!

Emily Help me get into the House of Commons!

Mary I ——

[**Mary** *is about to answer when there are sounds of boots in St Stephen's Hall above*]

Mary Too late, Miss. [*With purpose*] Have you got your speech?

Emily Yes: here [*points to her bag*] and *here* [*points to head*]

Mary Ready?

Emily Ready.

[**Mary** *picks up a wooden box that says* Pears Soap *on the side*]

Mary Then do it for me, now. [**Mary** *places box DSC, collects hat from chair*] Do it for Daisy [**Mary** *hands* **Emily** *her hat which she puts on and helps* **Emily** *onto the box*] Do it for us.

[**Mary** *moves into audience or to the side of the stage and listens*]

Emily Gentlemen of the House of Commons, do justice to the women of England by passing the Women's Enfranchisement Bill in 1911. The women of Australia were given the vote in King Edward's coronation year; give the women of England a similar right on the coronation of King George and Queen Mary. Queen Mary is British born, and if votes were given to women in the year of her coronation they would bear a special mark of appreciation.

For too long British women have been overlooked and ignored, their vital contribution to society disregarded.

We are denied the basic right to choose, have a say, to take part in the shaping of our Country. Why is it that half the population of this land is ignored?

Women are the core – we are *required* – the life-blood of this nation – without us there will be no future. We are mothers, we raise our families, go out to work, pay our taxes, carry out our civic duties in good faith. University graduates, teachers, doctors, lawyers, servants, mill-workers, cleaners – in all walks of life women are there – necessary and indispensable.

There are women working under this very roof, in Parliament, who are unheard and unseen – invisible – ghost women! You will not have noticed them, but they are there in the shadows – the Angels of the House. These women prepare your meals, wash your floors, build your fires to keep you warm. These women are enablers, they make the work of government possible.

Why should their sacrifice be ignored, why should *we* be denied a voice? Gentlemen of the House, a new dawn is breaking! For this generation and generations to come.

Do justice to the women of England! The answer lies in your hands . . .

[*Noises from St Stephen's Hall above and from outside the undercroft. The door is unlocked*]

Constable [*offstage, shouting*] Who's down there?

Emily [*shouting*] My name is Emily Wilding Davison. [*Police whistle sounds, clatter of boots down the steps*] I am a suffragette [*faces front*] and it is my *ambition* to enter the House!

[*Blackout*

[The March of the Women *plays*